VISTA

AMERICAN SIGN LANGUAGE SERIES
FUNCTIONAL NOTIONAL APPROACH

SIGNING
Naturally

STUDENT
WORKBOOK

L E V E L

1

EDITED BY LISA CAHN

DawnSignPress

San Diego, California

Edited by *Lisa Cahn*
Illustrations by *Chuck Baird, Patricia Pearson, Valerie Winemiller*
Sign Illustrations by *Frank Allen Paul, Paul Setzer*

Sign Models

Sandra Ammons   Ben Bahan   Tina Jo Breindel   Sue Burnes

Amanda Cervi   Bob Hiltermann   Anthony Kolombatovic   Ken Mikos   Erin Paul

John Reid   In Hwa Reisig

Published by DawnSignPress

ISBN: 0-915035-20-0

Printed in the United States of America

25   24   23

Quantity discounts and special purchase arrangements for teachers,
schools and bookstores are available. For more information, contact:

DawnSignPress
6130 Nancy Ridge Drive, San Diego, CA 92121-3223
(858) 625-0600 • Fax: (858) 625-2336
Toll Free: 1-800-549-5350   www.dawnsign.com

TABLE OF CONTENTS

INTRODUCTION

The *Signing Naturally: Student Videotext* and *Workbook - Level I* is designed to give you a way to review and practice what you learn in the classroom. With videotape, you can see the movement of signs as they are used in a sentence, observe how a sign form is influenced by the sign that precedes or follows, and learn how sign movements can be modified to change meaning. You can see when and how facial expressions occur and how body, head, and eye movements are used for phrasing and agreement. Most important, you see how language is used in context.

Each of the twelve units in Level 1 revolves around a major language function such as introducing oneself, asking for and giving information, asking for and giving directions, making requests, talking about activities, and identifying others. Through this functional approach, the language you learn is the language used in everyday conversation. By learning language functions in interactive contexts, you also develop conversational skills in confirming and correcting information, expressing degrees of uncertainty, and asking for clarification and repetition.

There are also two Cumulative Review units in Level 1 which focus on specific language and cultural behaviors. You will learn appropriate ways of getting attention, negotiating a signing environment, interrupting conversations, and learn phrases to ask for repetition and to close conversations.

Design of the *Videotext* and *Workbook*

The *Student Workbook* is designed to be a guide to the *Videotext*. Read the instructions in the workbook before beginning each videotaped activity. Then go back to the workbook for additional activities and readings.

The units are divided into several sections:

1) **LANGUAGE IN ACTION**: Each unit begins with videotaped conversations which are accompanied (in the workbook) by cued dialogues highlighting specific language functions and key phrases. You may see signs or expressions that are unfamiliar. Because of this, we suggest you approach the conversations in the following stages:

   a) Read the situation at the beginning of each cued dialogue in the workbook.
   b) View the conversation and try to follow the intent of the exchange. Do not concern yourself with individual unfamiliar signs.
   c) Read the cued dialogue in the workbook to see if you understood the exchange.
   d) View the conversation again, looking for how key phrases are expressed.
   e) Rehearse the key phrases.

The Conversation Practice section gives you an opportunity to rehearse the key phrases and conversation behaviors with a partner, in situations similar to the ones on screen. To keep it interesting and spontaneous, vary the conversation by adding personal information.

2) GRAMMAR NOTES: Grammar features are introduced as needed to express specific language functions. Grammar Notes provide a brief explanation of these features and are usually followed by a videotaped demonstration.

3) GRAMMAR PRACTICE: The Grammar Practice videotaped segments focus on language forms and structures in a controlled context. Some of these activities begin with a demonstration of specific grammar features; these are followed by activities that require you to respond to questions, or identify, discriminate, or summarize, and fill in answers in your workbook. Additional Pair Practice activities usually follow, so that you can apply what you learned in conversations with a partner.

4) COMPREHENSION: Comprehension activities test your understanding of vocabulary and language functions that you have learned. Narratives are used to help you build your receptive skills, learn vocabulary through context, and develop strategies for figuring out meaning without understanding every sign. These activities also require you to demonstrate your comprehension by filling in your workbook.

5) CULTURE/LANGUAGE NOTES: To understand language, you must understand its cultural context. The Culture/Language Notes provide you with a broad overview of the history, values, and social norms of the Deaf community.

6) VOCABULARY REVIEW: At the end of each unit in the workbook, you will find sign illustrations of key phrases and vocabulary for that unit. Many of the sign illustrations have a corresponding picture to show the meaning of the sign. Other more abstract vocabulary whose meaning cannot easily be illustrated with pictures are grouped into categories to help you remember the meaning of the sign. We chose not to give you English equivalents because they often restrict your understanding and usage of the signs.

Some signs vary from one region to the next. Your instructor may have introduced a different sign more commonly used in your local area than the one used in your workbook. Be sure to remember the local sign, but be aware that there will be different signs used in other parts of the United States and Canada.

An Answer Key is provided at the back so that you can check your answers.

How to Use the *Videotext* and *Workbook*

1) Since as much videotape time as possible has been used for language purposes, all instructions for videotaped activities are given in the workbook. Remember to read the instructions in the workbook before starting each activity.

2) Most activities on videotape allow a two- to three-second pause for you to mark your answers. This may not be enough time, so feel free to stop the tape to give yourself more time to answer. Avoid using the Pause button as this can cause damage to your tape.

3) If you miss a sign or sentence while working on an activity, don't rewind the tape to see just that part again, but continue the activity till the end, then replay the whole activity to complete the answers you missed. This way, you save time by not having to rewind repeatedly, and it saves wear and tear on the tape.

4) After you complete a workbook activity, you can replay the tape for additional language practice. For example, after identifying sentence types, go back and practice signing the sentences.

5) Use the *Videotext* as a reference to review and practice what you have learned, to prepare for tests, and to retain your Sign Language skills during breaks in school sessions.

Strategies for Learning American Sign Language

To increase your language learning in the classroom, develop the following habits:

1) Follow all conversations whether they are between the teacher and class, teacher and student, or student and student.

2) Focus on the signer's face, not on the hands. Don't break eye contact while in a signed conversation.

3) Develop active listening behaviors, i.e., nodding, responding with "huh?" "wow," "really?" Your teacher may stop to repeat information because you do not nod to indicate you are following along. This is not teacher/student behavior - it is cultural. Listeners have very active roles in signed conversations.

4) Participate as much as possible by adding comments, agreeing or disagreeing, etc. The more you participate, the more you will retain what you learn. Don't worry about mistakes. They are part of the learning process.

5) Try not to worry about a sign you missed. Work on getting the gist of the conversation. If a particular sign pops up over and over, and you haven't a clue to its meaning, then ask the teacher. Try to avoid asking your classmate for a quick English translation. You would lose out on valuable communication experiences that can strengthen your comprehension skills.

6) Leave English (and your voice) outside the door. Try not to translate in your head as you watch someone sign. Don't worry about memorizing, as repetition and context will help you acquire the language.

7) Try to maintain a signing environment during class breaks, before class begins, and whenever Deaf people are present.

8) Try not to miss class, especially at the beginning. Your class strives to form a language community; the cohesiveness of the group influences how rich the language exchange is in the classroom. Missing class makes it difficult to achieve this interactive environment.

DEAF AWARENESS QUIZ

Instruction: Circle the best answer (some will have more than one).

1. What is American Sign Language (ASL)? (circle two answers)

    a) a code similar to Braille
    b) a shortened form of English
    c) a language incorporating a lot of mime
    d) a language capable of expressing any abstract idea
    e) a language using picture-like images to express ideas and concepts
    f) a language utilizing space and movement to convey meaning

2. Historically, American Sign Language is related to:

    a) British Sign Language
    b) Swedish Sign Language
    c) French Sign Language
    d) German Sign Language

3. American Sign Language is used by most Deaf people in which of the following countries? (circle all that apply)

    a) Canada
    b) United States
    c) Mexico
    d) Brazil

4. What percent of Deaf people have Deaf parents?

    a) 10 percent
    b) 25 percent
    c) 50 percent
    d) 75 percent
    e) 90 percent

5. American Sign Language and Deaf culture are transmitted to Deaf people from generation to generation primarily through:

    a) family
    b) Deaf adults in the community
    c) residential Schools for the Deaf
    d) Sign Language teachers

6. The role of facial expressions, head movements, and eye gaze in American Sign Language is primarily:

    a) grammatical
    b) stylistic
    c) emotive
    d) attention getting

7. While watching another person sign, it is appropriate to focus on the signer's:

    a) hands
    b) chest area
    c) face

8. Among ASL signers, fingerspelling is mainly used in what ways? (circle all that apply)

    a) interchangeably with any sign
    b) to specify brand names
    c) as an artistic form of signing
    d) to give names of people and places

9. ASL makes use of the space in front of a signer's body to: (circle all that apply)

    a) indicate sentence types
    b) convey distance
    c) contrast two people, places, things, or ideas
    d) express time concepts

10. To get the attention of a Deaf person who is looking the other way, you should:

    a) yell as loud as you can
    b) tap him/her on the shoulder
    c) wave in his/her face
    d) go around and stand in front of the person

11. If your path is blocked by two signers conversing with each other, you should:

    a) wait until they stop talking before you pass through
    b) bend down very low in order to avoid passing through their signing space
    c) go ahead and walk through
    d) find another path

12. Which of the following are considered rude by Deaf people? (circle two answers)

    a) touching a person to get attention
    b) looking at a signed conversation without indicating you know Sign Language
    c) describing a distinctive feature of a person to identify him/her
    d) talking without signing in the presence of Deaf people

13. In general, the least effective communication strategy between Deaf and hearing people is:

    a) speech and lipreading
    b) using Sign Language
    c) writing back and forth
    d) using interpreters

14. Which of the following are valued in the Deaf community? (circle all that apply)

    a) for Deaf people to govern their own affairs
    b) being kept informed about the community and its members
    c) restoration of hearing loss
    d) group cohesiveness
    e) individualism

15. Other than the word "deaf," a culturally appropriate way to identify Deaf people would be to say they are:

    a) deaf and dumb
    b) deaf mutes
    c) hearing impaired
    d) all of the above
    e) none of the above

16. Historically, Deaf people have faced discrimination in the following areas:

    a) job hiring and promotion
    b) obtaining a driver's license without restrictions
    c) getting fair insurance rates
    d) getting decent housing
    e) obtaining access to public services, information, and entertainment

17. Some of the issues the National Association of the Deaf has fought for are: (circle all that apply)

    a) using Sign Language in the classroom
    b) maintaining a high proportion of Deaf teachers at the elementary and secondary levels
    c) the right of Deaf people to adopt children
    d) giving double tax exemption to Deaf people

18. What was the purpose of the protest rally at Gallaudet University in March 1988?

    a) to improve interpreting services
    b) to give priority to Sign Language research
    c) to assure that Deaf people be placed in top level decision-making positions
    d) to mainstream more hearing students at the University

As you go through this workbook and read the Grammar and Culture/Language Notes, you will find the correct answers to the questions above.

Unit 1
Introducing Oneself

LANGUAGE IN ACTION

Conversation 1

A participant at a conference (B) gives his name to the person at the registration desk (A).

A: greet B, **ask for name**
B: spell out name (Jon Keily)
A: (look up in file) spell name to confirm
B: **correct A**
A: (check file again) repeat spelling to confirm
B: **confirm**
A: respond (give registration packet)
B: express thanks

Conversation 2

Another person (A) bumps into Jon (B), the participant who just picked up his registration packet.

A: (recognize Jon) **spell out Jon's name to confirm**
B: **confirm**
A: (react) identify self
B: spell A's last name to confirm
A: **confirm**
A and B: greet each other

Key phrases that express target language functions are highlighted. Replay the videotape until you can follow the conversations without the aid of the cues. Then rehearse both conversations, especially the key phrases.

CONVERSATION PRACTICE

To practice the key phrases in a new context, find a partner and role play the situations below:

> **Situation 1:** You are responsible for getting the correct spelling of the names about to be printed on a program. Check the spelling of your partner's name, but when you ask, spell the name with one incorrect letter.
>
> **Situation 2:** You meet a friend you haven't seen in five years, but you are not sure of the person's name.

1

GRAMMAR PRACTICE

Same or Different

You will see two signers on screen. Both of them will sign something. If what they sign is the same, circle "S" below; if it is different, circle "D." Continue straight through the whole activity, then rewind and go through again for the ones you missed.

Sentences: Determine whether or not they sign the same sentence.

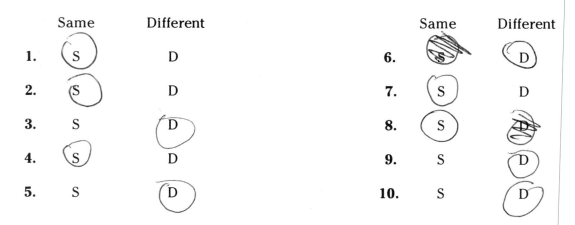

	Same	Different		Same	Different
1.	Ⓢ	D	6.	~~S~~	Ⓓ
2.	Ⓢ	D	7.	Ⓢ	D
3.	S	Ⓓ	8.	Ⓢ	~~D~~
4.	Ⓢ	D	9.	S	Ⓓ
5.	S	Ⓓ	10.	S	Ⓓ

Shapes: Determine whether or not they describe the same shape.

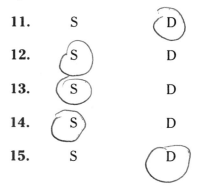

11.	S	Ⓓ
12.	Ⓢ	D
13.	Ⓢ	D
14.	Ⓢ	D
15.	S	Ⓓ

Sequences of Shapes: Determine whether or not they describe the shapes in the same sequence.

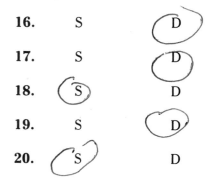

16.	S	Ⓓ
17.	S	Ⓓ
18.	Ⓢ	D
19.	S	Ⓓ
20.	Ⓢ	D

Answers on page 176.

CULTURE/LANGUAGE NOTES

Introduction to American Sign Language

Many people mistakenly believe that American Sign Language (ASL) is English conveyed through signs. Some think that it is a manual code for English, that it can express only concrete information, or that there is one universal sign language used by Deaf people around the world.

Linguistic research demonstrates, however, that ASL is comparable in complexity and expressiveness to spoken languages. It is not a form of English. It has its own distinct grammatical structure, which must be mastered in the same way as the grammar of any other language. ASL differs from spoken languages in that it is visual rather than auditory and is composed of precise handshapes and movements.

ASL is capable of conveying subtle, complex, and abstract ideas. Signers can discuss philosophy, literature, or politics as well as football, cars or income taxes. Sign Language can express poetry as poignantly as can any spoken language and can communicate humor, wit, and satire just as bitingly. As in other languages, new vocabulary items are constantly being introduced by the community in response to cultural and technological change.

ASL is not universal. Just as hearing people in different countries speak different languages, so do Deaf people around the world sign different languages. Deaf people in Mexico use a different sign language from that used in the U.S. Because of historical circumstances, contemporary ASL is more like French Sign Language than like British Sign Language.

ASL was developed by American Deaf people to communicate with each other and has existed as long as there have been Deaf Americans. Standardization was begun in 1817 when Laurent Clerc and Thomas H. Gallaudet established the first School for the Deaf in the U.S. Students afterwards spread the use of ASL to other parts of the U.S. and Canada. Traditionally, the language has been passed from one generation to the next in the residential school environment, especially through dormitory life. Even when signs were not permitted in the classroom, the children of Deaf parents, as well as Deaf teachers and staff, would secretly pass on the language to other students. ASL is now used by approximately one-half million Deaf people in the U.S. and Canada.

Since the late 1800's, Deaf people have been discouraged from using ASL. Many well-meaning but misguided educators, believing that the only way for deaf people to fit into the hearing world is through speech and lipreading, have insisted that deaf children try to learn to speak English. Some have even gone so far as to tie down deaf children's hands to prevent them from signing. Despite these and other attempts to discourage signing, ASL continues to be the preferred language of the Deaf community. Far from seeing the use of sign as a handicap, Deaf people regard ASL as their natural language which reflects their cultural values and keeps their traditions and heritage alive. In this class, you will see how ASL has shaped and is shaped by the culture of Deaf Americans.

Introduction to the Deaf Community

In the spring of 1988, student protesters at Gallaudet University in Washington, D.C. sent a loud and clear message to the world: "Prejudice is believing that deaf people have to be taken care of."

Gallaudet trustees had set the spark for this campus protest by ignoring the wishes of Deaf students that a Deaf person be chosen as the 124-year-old college's seventh president. Instead, the trustees chose as president a person who is not only hearing, but also unable to communicate in Sign Language. Students erupted in a rage. They boycotted classes and blockaded entrances to the college signing "Deaf Power." The protest quickly mushroomed into a national debate over the civil rights of Deaf people. The students received support from Deaf communities around the world. The reason is that Gallaudet, which was founded by an act of Congress in 1864, has become one of the world's foremost educational centers for Deaf people. Yet it has never had a Deaf president - the result, said students and staff, of the paternalism of the hearing world that perpetuates the myth that Deaf people cannot function on their own.

Faced with such opposition, the newly appointed president resigned, a Deaf chairperson of the Board of Trustees was appointed and, three days later, the board voted to hire as president, I. King Jordan, the former dean of the College of Arts and Science, a Gallaudet graduate with a Ph.D. in Psychology.

That night, the new president, the chairperson of the Board of Trustees, and the student body president talked about the future of the 2,123-student university. As the three emerged from the president's office, the teary-eyed student body president said, "There was no interpreter." None was needed because for the first time in the school's history, Deaf people held the fate of the nation's only university for the Deaf in their own hands.

During this eight-day protest, Deaf students demanded that the hearing world respect their right to govern their own lives. They showed that deafness is not a disability, but rather the quality that unites Deaf people into a cohesive, vibrant community. At the heart of this community is its language, ASL. This language embodies the thoughts, experiences, traditions, and values shared by the community. Deaf people themselves are poets, carpenters, mechanics, farmers, artists, teachers, ministers, lawyers, business people and journalists. Deaf people have their own community organizations, professional associations, theatres, and churches. And as the hearing world learned, the Deaf community has its own leaders.

A note on terminology. Over the years, different terms have been used to refer to Deaf people. Some older terms are offensive today and should be avoided, especially "deaf and dumb" and "deaf mute." The term "hearing impaired" is often used by public institutions and political groups as an inclusive term to refer to all people with any degree of hearing loss. This term, however, does not distinguish between people with hearing loss and Deaf people. Deaf people, because of their language and cultural identity, prefer to be called "Deaf."

End of Unit I

KEY PHRASES

Ask for name

Express pleasure in meeting someone

VOCABULARY REVIEW

WH-WORD
QUESTION SIGNS

SAME/
DIFFERENT

DRAW/WRITE

Unit 2
Exchanging Personal Information

LANGUAGE IN ACTION

Conversation 1

Lynne (A), a Sign Language student, approaches Ben (B) to ask the time.

A: ask for time (speaking)
B: gesture that you can't hear
A: ask if deaf (signing)
B: affirm, **ask if deaf**
A: reply negatively, **explain that you're learning Sign Language**
B: ask where
A: tell where
B: respond, **ask who A's teacher is**
A: fingerspell name of teacher
B: express uncertainty, describe person to confirm
A: confirm
B: acknowledge
A: ask the time
B: (show watch)
A: explain you're late for class, **begin conversation closing**
B: close conversation

Conversation 2

Cinnie (A) asks her friend Flo (B) about someone else in the room.

A: (point to the other person) **ask if person is deaf**
B: **respond negatively, tell that she is hearing**
A: **ask if she is a student**
B: **respond affirmatively**, tell that she is learning Sign Language, and identify her teacher by name sign
A: repeat name sign, ask who
B: fingerspell name
A: **respond**

Key phrases that express target language functions are highlighted. Replay the videotape until you can follow the conversations without the aid of the cues. Then rehearse both conversations, especially the key phrases.

CONVERSATION PRACTICE

To practice the key phrases in a new context, find a partner and role play the situations below:

> **Situation 1:** You join your friend at a table in the cafeteria. Point out other people in the room and ask questions about them.
>
> **Situation 2:** You are waiting in the checkout line at a grocery store. You realize the person standing in front of you is Deaf - you have seen him/her somewhere before. Introduce yourself.

GRAMMAR NOTES

Forming Questions

You may have noticed your teacher using a lot of facial expressions and head movements while s/he signs. These are called "non-manual behaviors," and they not only show affect or emotion, but also have grammatical functions. Just as speakers of English use vocal intonation to mark sentence types, signers use non-manual behaviors to ask a question, make a negative statement, or to emphasize a point. In this unit, we focus on the non-manual behaviors used for yes/no and wh-word questions.

A **yes/no question** requires a simple yes or no answer. For example, "Do you have children?" or "Do you like coffee?" To ask a yes/no question, a signer should do the following:

1) raise eyebrows (widen eyes)
2) lean head forward
3) hold the last sign in the sentence

For example:

(Is s/he deaf?)

A **wh-word question** asks who, what, where, when, etc., and requires a statement for an answer. To ask a wh-word question, a signer should do the following:

1) lower eyebrows
2) lean head forward
3) hold the last sign in the sentence (usually a wh-word sign)

For example:

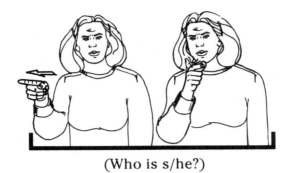

(Who is s/he?)

You will see Ella modeling these two question forms at the beginning of the next activity.

NOTE: When watching someone sign, you should focus on the signer's face. Vital information is conveyed by non-manual behaviors, and by missing facial expressions, you could miss the signer's intent. Avoid the tendency to focus on the signer's hands.

GRAMMAR PRACTICE

Question Types

On screen, Ella will model a yes/no question and a wh-word question. She will then sign ten questions, preceded by an example. Indicate whether each one is a yes/no question or a wh-word question by circling the appropriate answer.

Example: (y/n) wh

1.   y/n   (wh)

2.   y/n   (wh)

3.   (y/n)   wh

4.   y/n   (wh)

5.   (y/n)   wh

6.   (y/n)   wh

7.   (y/n)   wh

8.   y/n   (wh)

9.   y/n   (wh)

10. (y/n)   wh

Check your answers on page 176. Then, rewind the tape to the beginning of this exercise and practice signing each sentence.

9

Numbers: 1- 10

On screen, Ron will model numbers 1-10. Notice where the palm of his hand is facing as he signs each number. Replay the tape and practice each number sign.

COMPREHENSION

Number Phrases

On screen, Brian and Mary will each sign five number phrases. Write down the numbers given in each phrase.

Example: __2__ , __1__

1. __7__ , __10__   6. __7__ , __6__
2. __1__ , __3__   7. __5__ , __4__
3. __6__ , __2__   8. __3__ , __8__
4. __3__ , __8__   9. __4__ , __7__
5. __10__ , __5__   10. __8__ , __9__

Answers on page 176.

CULTURE/LANGUAGE NOTES

Which Hand Do I Use?

All signers have a dominant and a non-dominant hand. If you are right-handed, use your right hand as dominant; if left-handed, use your left hand as dominant. If you are ambidextrous, you should choose one hand as your dominant hand and be consistent with its use.

One-handed signs are formed with only one hand. Always use your dominant hand to sign these. For example:

Two-handed symmetrical signs require equal use of both dominant and nondominant hands in symmetrical movements. For example:

In **two-handed non-symmetrical signs**, the dominant hand moves while the nondominant hand remains stationary. For example:

Carefully observe how your Sign Language teacher forms each sign as s/he introduces it. Be sure you are consistent in the use of your dominant hand.

End of Unit 2

KEY PHRASES

Ask if deaf

Correct information (tell you are hearing)

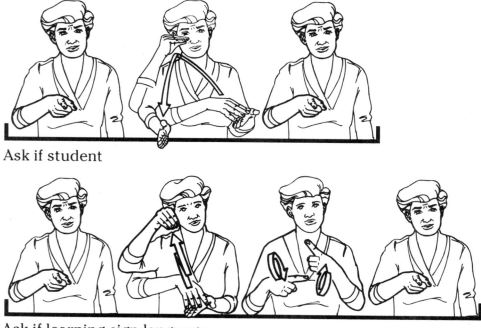

Ask if student

Ask if learning sign language

12

Ask where person is studying sign language

VOCABULARY REVIEW

IDENTIFYING PEOPLE

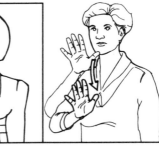

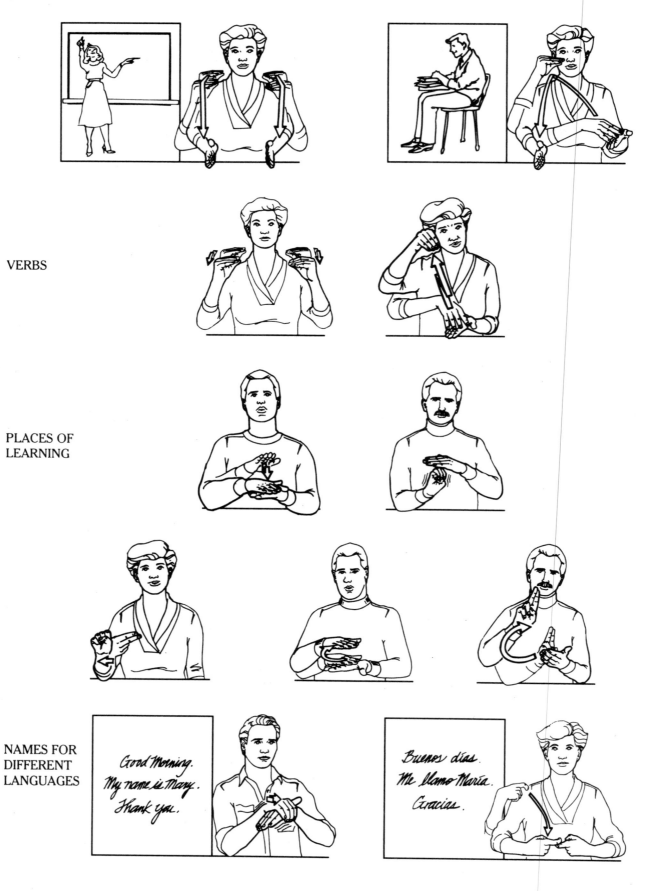

VERBS

PLACES OF
LEARNING

NAMES FOR
DIFFERENT
LANGUAGES

Good Morning.
My name is Mary.
Thank you.

Buenos días.
Me llamo María.
Gracias.

RESPONSES

MEMORY
(opposites)

FAMILIARITY
(opposites)

COMMANDS

Noun   Verbs

NUMBERS
1 –10

Unit 3
Talking About Surroundings

LANGUAGE IN ACTION

Conversation 1

Ben (A) approaches Brian (B) to ask where to get some coffee.

A: ask if B is drinking coffee
B: reply negatively, tell what you are drinking
A: respond, explain you want some coffee, **ask where** you can buy it
B: tell where
A: repeat directions to confirm
B: confirm
A: tell B you're going there now and will be back
B: respond, say goodbye

Conversation 2

Ellen (A), a Sign Language student, approaches Mary (B) to ask where the telephone is.

A: ask where the telephone is
B: tell where
A: ask if near elevator
B: correct, give additional information
A: check directions to confirm
B: confirm
A: express thanks
B: say goodbye

Key phrases that express target language functions are highlighted. Replay the videotape until you can follow the conversations without the aid of the cues. Then rehearse both conversations, especially the key phrases.

CONVERSATION PRACTICE

To practice the key phrases in a new context, find a partner and role play the situations below:

Situation 1: Explain that you want to buy _____. Ask your partner for directions. (Possible items to buy: food, drink, tea, milk, coffee, soda pop, candy.)

Situation 2: Ask your partner where _____ is located. Confirm the directions given. (Possible locations: water fountain, telephone, teacher's office, classroom, library, bookstore.)

GRAMMAR NOTES

Spatial Agreement

To give directions in ASL, you need to use the signing space in front of you and particular non-manual behaviors to correlate with the actual environment. First, give general information by pointing in the direction of the place, then give specific directions, giving enough information that the listener can visualize the route or location you describe. You need to develop skills with your eyes, face and hands to show relative distance, trace the actual route to follow, and indicate direction of turns and location of landmarks.

Eye Gaze/Location Agreement. Eye gaze should "agree with" the route you trace, that is, you should visualize the places along the route, and shift your eye gaze to "look at" the places you describe. You should also tilt your head to the right as you indicate a location on the left (i.e., as if looking at the location), and tilt your head to the left to indicate a location on your right.

Conveying Distance. You can indicate relative distance with specific non-manual behaviors. These non-manuals are the same whether you're talking about where to turn in a hallway or the distance between cities. That is, the categories of "far away," "moderate distance," or "very near" do not specify actual distance, but rather are relative to the locations you're talking about.

To show that a location is **far away**, do the following:

1) tilt head (in agreement with direction)
2) squint eyes
3) open mouth slightly
4) trace route: extend arm fully

To show **moderate distance**, do the following:

1) tilt head (in agreement with direction)
2) purse lips slightly
3) trace route: extend arm moderately

To show that a location is **very near**, do the following:

1) tilt head (in agreement with direction)
2) "cs" behavior (for cheek to shoulder): clench teeth, turn head to the dominant side, with cheek almost touching shoulder
3) trace route: keep hand close to body (do not extend arm)

Ella will model these non-manual behaviors for showing relative distance at the beginning of the next activity.

NOTE: If you're standing face to face with a signer giving directions, you should try to visualize the locations from **the signer's perspective**.

GRAMMAR PRACTICE

Conveying Distance: Tracing Routes

On screen, Ella will demonstrate the non-manual behaviors for showing relative distance: far away, moderate distance, and very near. Then she and Ben will show how to trace the routes indicated in the picture below. Try to visualize the directions from the signer's perspective. If you have difficulty, position yourself next to but facing away from the screen, so that your perspective is the same as the signer's.

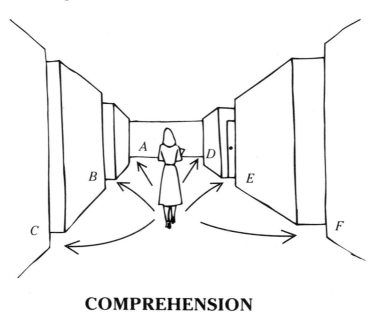

COMPREHENSION

Identify Where

Ella will tell the locations of six different places or things. After she signs each sentence, stop the videotape and write the name of the place in the correct location on the illustration below. Ella begins with an example, telling the location of the water fountain.

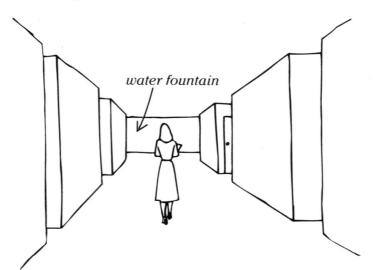

water fountain

Answers on page 176.

Picture It

Five people will each describe a picture that includes shapes and numbers. Visualize the picture as it's being described. After each description, stop the tape and draw as accurately as possible the picture described.

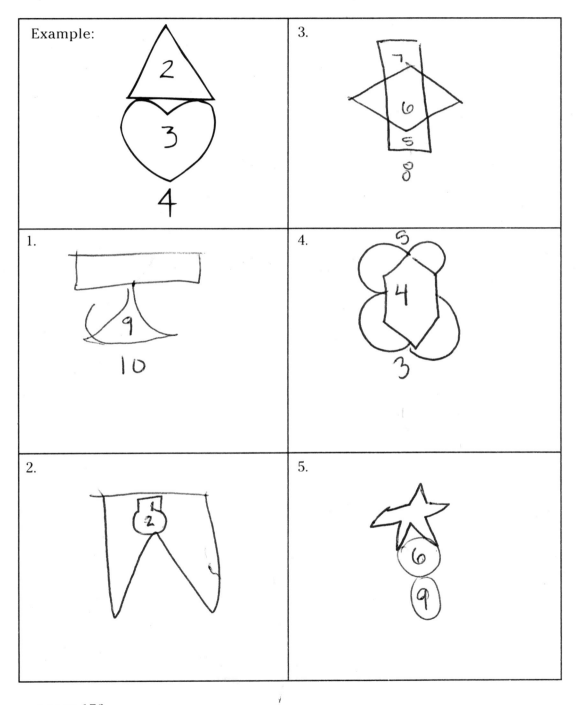

Answers on page 176.

Fingerspelling, Part 1

On screen Brian, Cinnie, and Ron will each spell a word. Two of the three words are the same. Identify the person who spells a different word by checking the appropriate box below. They will first give an example.

	Brian	Cinnie	Ron
Example:	☐	☑	☐
1.	☒	☐	☐
2.	☐	☐	☒
3.	☐	☒	☐
4.	☐	☐	☒
5.	☒	☐	☐
6.	☒	☐	☐
7.	☐	☒	☐
8.	☐	☐	☒
9.	☐	☒	☐
10.	☐	☒	☐

Answers on page 176.

PAIR PRACTICE

Practice fingerspelling two-letter combinations until you feel comfortable making the transition between the two letters:

ba, be, bo	el, fl, sl	an, en, on
pt, po, pa	tr, cr, ar	ay, oy, ei

Fingerspell one combination from each set to your partner, and have him/her write down the letters. Afterwards, check that your partner got the letter combinations right.

End of Unit 3

KEY PHRASES

Ask where restroom is

Tell where (near the water fountain)

Respond (tell you will be right back)

Ask where you can buy coffee

23

VOCABULARY REVIEW

PLACES AND THINGS
AROUND THE CLASSROOM

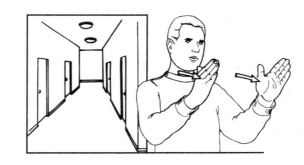

SNACKS

VERBS

TELL LOCATIONS

RESPOND
Indicate the information is wrong

OBJECTS

Unit 4
Telling Where You Live

LANGUAGE IN ACTION

Conversation 1

Lon (A), visiting from out of state, attends a party where he introduces himself to Michelle (B), a Sign Language student.

    A: introduce self, ask name
    B: give name (Jane)
    A: ask if learning Sign Language
    B: respond affirmatively, point to person in room, and tell that he's your teacher
    A: ask if teacher is deaf
    B: respond affirmatively
    A: ask where class is
    B: give name of college; tell where
    A: ask where B lives
    B: tell where
    A: respond, **ask if B walks to class** everyday
    B: respond affirmatively, **tell that you ride a bicycle** sometimes
    A: respond, **ask if B bicycled** to the party
    B: respond negatively (you came by bus)
    A: respond

Conversation 2

(Scene continues from Conversation 1 above)

    B: ask where A lives
    A: tell where
    B: (you don't recognize the sign for where he lives) **ask what it means**
    A: describe something associated with that place, ask if B knows where you mean
    B: respond, repeat the sign to confirm
    A: confirm
    B: ask how A came here
    A: tell how
    B: respond (someone else interrupts, gets A's attention)
    A: excuse yourself, begin conversation closing
    B: close conversation

Key phrases that express target language functions are highlighted. Replay the videotape until you can follow the conversations without the aid of the cues. Then rehearse both conversations, especially the key phrases.

CONVERSATION PRACTICE

To practice the key phrases in a new context, find a partner and role play the situations below:

Situation 1: You are attending a workshop with Sign Language students from various programs. Introduce yourself and exchange information about each other's Sign Language program.

Situation 2: Ask and tell each other where you live. Pick a city that can be identified or described using both gestures and signs. Have your partner guess what city/state you're from. (For example, Texas: 10-gallon hat; Seattle: Space Needle; New York: Statue of Liberty; Las Vegas: slot machines; San Francisco: Golden Gate Bridge, hills; Hawaii: hula dancing.)

GRAMMAR PRACTICE

Numbers 11-20

Flo will model numbers 11-20. Notice how numbers 11-15 are formed: in 11 and 12 the fingers flick off the thumb while in 13, 14 and 15 the fingers bend at the knuckle. For all numbers 11-15, the palm faces the body and the movement is repeated.

Numbers 16-19 are a blend of the numbers 10 and 6, 7, 8, or 9. Notice how the transition between the two numbers is made with a twist of the wrist. (This form varies in different regions of the U.S. and Canada.)

Replay the tape and practice each number sign.

Spatial Referencing: Grid 1-6

For each grid that follows, a signer will demonstrate how to identify the square(s) marked with an X. Notice how the signers use the following sequence:

- set and hold a reference point (using raised eyebrows)
- identify correct square (using raised eyebrows)
- give instructions where the X is located

Notice also how the signers' eye gaze and use of space correlate with the visualized grid.

Grid 1.

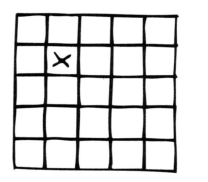

Grid 4.

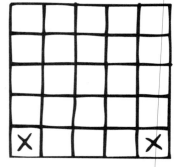

Grid 2.

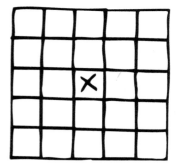

Grid 5.

Grid 3.

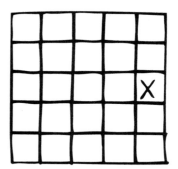

Grid 6.

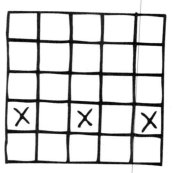

Now you try it. Rewind the tape and rehearse with each signer.

PAIR PRACTICE

Draw your own 20-square grid on a blank sheet of paper. Select ten of the squares and number them. Find a partner and sign the location and number of each of the squares you selected; have your partner write the numbers in the corresponding squares of his/her own grid. When watching your partner sign, remember to visualize the locations from the signer's perspective.

COMPREHENSION

Grid Game

Ken will identify one of the squares in the following grid and tell you what is located there. Stop the videotape after each instruction, find the picture of what's in that square (see below), and write the letter corresponding to the picture in the correct location. Ken will first sign an example – see how it is marked in the grid. Remember to use the signer's perspective.

a.

b.

c.

d.

e.

f.

g.   h.   i.   j.   k

Answers on page 177.

Ben's Keys

Ben has just lost his keys. Luckily, Cinnie found them. On screen, you will see Ben and Cinnie talk about the keys. After watching this segment, answer the questions below.

1. How many keys does Ben have altogether? _____ 12 _____

2. What are the keys for, and how many does he have for each purpose?

for: _____ 5 _____ how many? _____ apartment _____

for: _____ 1 _____ how many? _____ padlock _____

for: _____ 3 _____ how many? _____ car _____

for: _____ 1 _____ how many? _____ bike _____

for: _____ 2 _____ how many? _____ work _____

3. Where did Cinnie find the keys? _____ classroom _____

4. In what city does Ben live? _____ New York _____

Answers on page 177.

Trivia #1

Who was the first Deaf teacher in America?

To find the answer, you have to solve a series of addition problems. The answer to each problem will give you one letter of the person's name.

Brian will give you two numbers to add. A letter will appear on screen at the same time. Figure out the sum, find the sum below, and above it write in the letter that appears on screen.

Brian will first give an example.

Answer:

E	R	C	N	E	A	L	R	T	L	U	C
18	20	15	27	17	23	16	24	25	21	22	29

This person helped found the first state School for the Deaf in America in Hartford, Connecticut in 1817. A memorial has been erected in his honor at the school and also at Gallaudet University in Washington, D.C. Some streets and buildings on the campuses of state Schools for the Deaf and at Gallaudet University have been named after him.

Answer on page 177.

CULTURE/LANGUAGE NOTES

When Do I Fingerspell?

When two languages co-exist in any community, the language of the majority culture may influence the language of the minority culture. One of the ways that ASL is influenced by English is the incorporation of certain fingerspelled English words.

In general, fingerspelling is used to give:

- names of people
- names of cities and states
- titles of movies or books
- brand names

Fingerspelling is also used for "fingerspelled loan signs." These are two- to five-letter, commonly used words that have their own unique patterns of movement. These movement patterns are different from ordinary fingerspelling: the words have become ASL signs rather than fingerspelled words. Some of these you may already know, i.e., OK, car, bus.

Strategies for Fingerspelling

1) When you see a fingerspelled word, try to **see the shape and movement pattern** of the word rather than trying to see each letter. Read the whole word as it is spelled just as you would read a printed word. (Also, try to keep your eyes on the signer's face while doing this.)

2) When you yourself fingerspell words, be sure to keep your hand **slightly to the right of your face, and below your chin** (or to the left if you are lefthanded). Keep your elbow down, close to your body, and your arm relaxed, as in the picture provided.

3) When you fingerspell, work on the flow of movement and the blend of handshapes in the whole word, rather than focusing on articulating each letter. **Avoid "bouncing" each letter.**

Remember that fingerspelling is **not a substitute for signing**. Do *not* spell a word as your first alternative for expressing an idea for which you don't know a sign. Instead, point, describe, act out, gesture, draw – anything but fingerspell.

End of Unit 4

KEY PHRASES

Ask where person lives

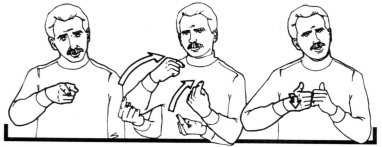

Ask how person got here

Tell how you got here

34

VOCABULARY REVIEW

HOUSING

TRANSPORTATION

TELL LOCATION

COLORS

**NUMBERS
11 – 20**

11

12

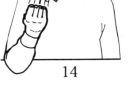

13

14

15

16

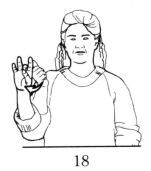

17

18

19

20

Unit 5
Talking About Your Family

LANGUAGE IN ACTION

Conversation 1

Ron is giving a party at his house. One of the guests, Mary (A), notices a wedding picture on a table and asks Ron (B) about the people in the picture.

A: ask B if the picture is of his family
B: respond affirmatively, explain that it's your brother's wedding
A: respond, **ask how many siblings**
B: tell how many, and identify self in picture
A: respond, comment about B's appearance
B: agree, identify other people in picture
A: ask if any are deaf
B: respond
A: respond, comment about the picture

Conversation 2

Flo (A) meets Ella (B) at a bookstore. They haven't seen each other for quite some time.

A and B: exchange greetings
A: exclaim how big B is, recall how small she was; **ask if married**
B: respond affirmatively, tell about your children
A: ask if children are deaf
B: respond affirmatively, ask about A's husband
A: respond (divorced)
B: make comment; **ask about children**
A: tell about children
B: respond, compliment A's appearance
A: return compliment

Key phrases that express target language functions are highlighted. Replay the videotape until you can follow the conversations without the aid of the cues. Then rehearse both conversations, especially the key phrases.

CONVERSATION PRACTICE

To practice the key phrases in a new context, find a partner and role play the situations below:

GRAMMAR NOTES

Situation 1: Have ready a couple of pictures of your brothers and sisters (or other family members).

You've just picked up your pictures from a photo lab. Approach a friend and show him/her the pictures. Identify each person in the pictures.

Situation 2: At a picnic sponsored by a local Deaf club, you introduce yourself to a person just after s/he has finished talking with someone.

After introducing yourself, ask if the person s/he just finished talking with is his/her spouse, if they have children, etc.

Contrastive Structure

When talking about people, places, or things ("referents") that are not in the immediate environment, it is important to establish these referents in specific locations in the signing space in front of you. Referents are established by naming what you are referring to and then designating (by pointing to) a location; they can be referred to again by simply pointing to the same location.

For example, if you have established David on your left and Scott on your right, you should retain the same points of reference as you continue talking about them. As you give additional information about David, point to the space on your left and give the information; it is not necessary to repeat the name, as pointing to that location means "David." Similarly, pointing to the space on your right means "Scott."

As you compare or contrast two people, places, or things, be sure to **shift your head and body slightly** in agreement with the space you established for each referent. If you point to the left, shift to the left; if you point to the right, shift to the right.

In the videotaped exercise that follows, Ben will use contrastive structure to talk about two different people.

GRAMMAR PRACTICE

Bob and Bill

On screen, Ben will contrast two good friends, Bob and Bill. On the next page, write down the information given about each person. There will be a brief pause between sentences. If you need more time, stop the tape.

Ben will give an example first.

Bob	Bill
Example: _____ likes candy _____	_____ likes soda _____

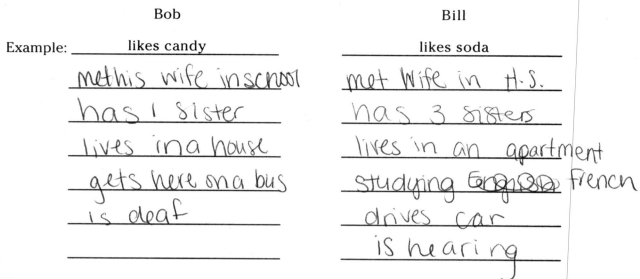

Bob:
- met his wife in school
- has 1 sister
- lives in a house
- gets here on a bus
- is deaf

Bill:
- met wife in H.S.
- has 3 sisters
- lives in an apartment
- studying ~~English~~ French
- drives car
- is hearing

Answers on page 177.

PAIR PRACTICE

Find a partner to practice with. Sign sentences comparing two of your friends, children or siblings. Use these topics:

names	mode of transportation	types of residence
marital status	deaf/hearing	color of car
number of children	education	
likes/preferences	residences	

Have your partner record what you said so you can check that s/he understood you.

GRAMMAR NOTES

Forming Negative Statements

To form a negative statement, use this sign:

Be sure to maintain a negative headshake throughout the statement.

To answer no to a yes/no question, use this sign:

This should be followed either by a negative statement as described above, or by a statement that gives the correct information. For example (in English), to answer the question "Are you married?", either use a negative statement ("No, I'm not married") or correct the information ("No, I'm divorced").

There is another sign used for certain kinds of negative statements:

In English you can use the word "no" to negate different kinds of statements. You can say, "I have no sisters," or "There is no ice cream left," or "There is no such thing." In ASL, however, to say you don't have something, or there is none, or something doesn't exist, use this sign to form the negative statement.

To practice these signs in negative responses, go on to the next activity.

GRAMMAR PRACTICE

Negative Responses

Mary will sign six questions. You are to sign two negative responses to each question:

1) negative statement
2) negating and correcting the information

Stop the videotape after each question and sign your responses. When you start the tape again, Ron and Cinnie will each demonstrate one type of negative response.

COMPREHENSION

Ten Years Later. . .

The newscaster on screen will give you the latest update on what has happened to the members of this family in the last ten years. Stop the tape after each segment and write the information given beside each family member pictured below.

dead

had ten kittens

dead

grown
in high school
has boyfriend

gave birth
to deaf boy
boy is 9 yrs old

married:
divorced
in college
studying
french

still living

studying ASL
bought house

Answers on page 177.

Fingerspelling, Part 2

Ken and Brian will sign ten sentences, each of which includes a fingerspelled name. Circle the name that is spelled.

Example: Pam (Pat) Kay

1.   Tim   Sam   (Tom)
2.   Eve   (Sue)   Ava
3.   (Ben)   Bev   Bea
4.   (Sean) Anne   Emma
5.   Noah   Nora   (Mona)
6.   Paul   (Kris)   Kirk
7.   (Judy)   Jody   Joey
8.   Jenna Jenny (Jesse)
9.   Glenn (Gregg) Glenda
10. Billy (Bobby) Barry

Answers on page 178.

Riddle

Watch Brian tell you a story on screen and answer the question at the end of the story.

Answer on page 178.   Bus driver made 5 stops

End of Unit 5

43

KEY PHRASES

Ask if married

Respond (not married)

Ask if have children

Respond (no children)

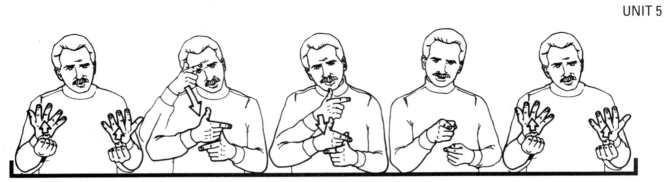

Ask how many brothers and sisters

Tell how many (2 brothers and 1 sister)

Ask if person lives alone

Ask who person lives with

VOCABULARY REVIEW

FAMILY MEMBERS

| Categories | Male | Female | Either |

EXTENDED FAMILY

Male   Female   Either

OTHER RELATIONSHIPS

Male	Female	Either

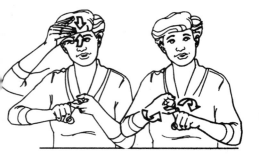
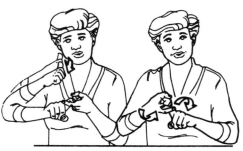

LIVING SITUATION

LIFE EVENTS
Verbs

PERSONAL PRONOUNS

POSSESSIVE PRONOUNS

NEGATION

Unit 6
Telling About Activities

LANGUAGE IN ACTION

Conversation 1

Ben (A) joins Cinnie (B) at lunch break at work.

A and B: greet each other
A: ask B what she will do next Friday
B: say you're not doing anything
A: make suggestion for Friday afternoon
B: (check calendar) **decline, explain why**, suggest an alternate day
A: agree, but suggest a later time
B: (check calendar) agree
A: respond
B: comment on food
A: agree

Conversation 2

Flo (A) is standing outside in front of a theatre waiting for Ken (B) who is somewhat late.

A: (waiting)
B: (finally arrive)
A: greet B
B: greet A, **apologize, explain why** you're late, ask if A waited a long time
A: reassure B, explain what you did while waiting; suggest you both go inside now
B: ask if A has tickets
A: (hand B one ticket)
A and B: (walk to door)

Key phrases that express target language functions are highlighted. Replay the videotape until you can follow the conversations without the aid of the cues. Then rehearse both conversations, especially the key phrases.

CONVERSATION PRACTICE

To practice the key phrases in a new context, find a partner and role play the situations below:

Situation 1: Approach your partner and suggest an activity in the near future. (Possible activities: movie, shopping, playing cards, playing basketball, cooking class.)
Your partner should ask you if s/he can bring along one or two family members (i.e., brothers, sisters, parents, grandparents, children, spouse). Settle on a date.

Situation 2: You and your friend agreed to meet at a restaurant at 11:30 for brunch. It is now 12:15. Approach your friend, apologize and explain your lateness. (Possible reasons: you overslept, couldn't find parking, couldn't find the restaurant, traffic, medical or dental appointment.)

GRAMMAR NOTES

Time Concepts

To indicate tense (past, present, future) in ASL, use a time sign at the **beginning** of the sentence. Once the tense has been established, everything that follows is understood to be in that time frame until a new time is specified.

To understand time signs, it may be helpful to imagine a **time line** as pictured below. Everything referring to the future moves forward; everything referring to the past moves back. Everything referring to the present is signed just in front of the body.

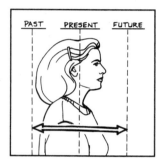

Here are some examples of time signs that reflect points on the time line:

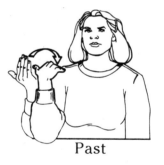  

| Past | Immediate Past ("yesterday") | Future | Immediate Future ("tomorrow") |

To refer to specific times, the general time signs for past, present, and future are combined with the signs for days, weeks, and months. That is, to sign the concept "last month," the sign for "past" is combined with the sign for "month." Another way to specify time is to incorporate number. That is, to sign the concept "in two weeks," the forward movement indicating future and the number two are both incorporated into the sign for "week."

For practice in understanding time signs, do the videotaped exercises that follow.

GRAMMAR PRACTICE

Calendar, Part 1

Mary will tell you about different activities that occurred or will occur within the month. After each statement, stop the tape and circle the appropriate date and part of day the activity occurred or will occur. For this activity, "today" is always *Wednesday the 16th*.

Example:

Answers on page 178.

Numbers: 21-30

Brian will model numbers 21- 30. Notice that the sign forms for 21 and 22 are different from 23-29. Replay the tape and practice each number sign.

COMPREHENSION

Main Street, USA

Ella will identify different buildings on Main Street, USA (see the illustration), and ask you questions. Stop the tape and write the answers below.

1. apt building

2. somersat apartment

3. church

4. Jack's steakhouse

5. hospital

6. sears

7. Jacks steak house

Answers on page 178.

PAIR PRACTICE

Using the picture below, practice asking and telling your partner what's located in various places, i.e., "what is next to the store?" or "what is across the street from the park?"

What Did They Decide?

In each of the three dialogues, Mary and Brian discuss what they will do in the near future. For each dialogue, circle the activity that was finally agreed upon, and write in the day the activity will take place.

Dialogue 1

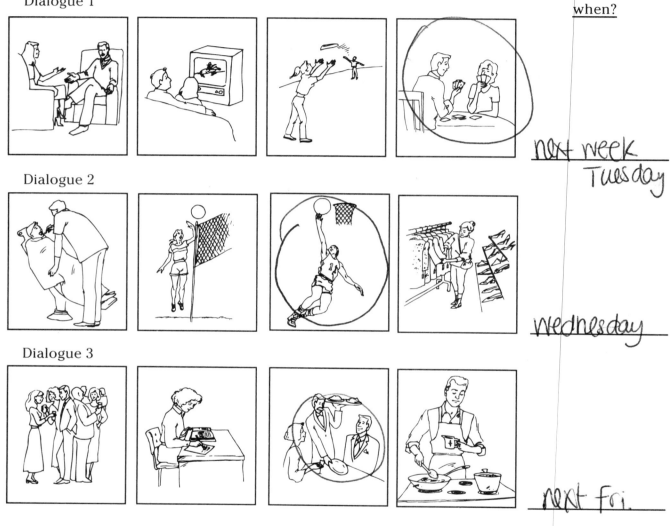

when?

next week
Tuesday

wednesday

next fri.

Answers on page 178.

What Reasons Did They Give?

In each of these dialogues, one of the two signers explains his absence or tardiness. For each dialogue, write in the reasons given.

Dialogue 4 – reasons given:

_____ sick, went to _____
_____ doctor's _____
_____

Dialogue 5 – reasons given:

_____ late, chatting with _____
_____ friends then there _____
_____ was traffic _____

Answers on page 178.

PAIR PRACTICE

To practice the activity vocabulary you have learned, ask your partner his/her opinion of the following:

babysitting
drinking coffee (coke, milk)
playing basketball (football, baseball)
studying
cleaning
cleaning house
work
watching a basketball game
riding a bicycle
exercising (aerobics, running, swimming)
weightlifting
getting up early in the morning
smoking
watching a movie
eating at McDonald's

Trivia #2

Who said, "Sign Language is God's noblest gift to the Deaf"?

To find the answer, you have to solve a series of subtraction problems. The answer to each problem will give you the location of one letter of the person's name.

Brian will sign a subtraction problem. Figure out the difference, then write the corresponding letter above that number in the answer key. (See the example below.)

Answer:

G e o r g e   V e d i t z

9 26 16 1 3 20   6 14 7 17 11 5

Clues:

Example:	1.	2.	3.	4.	5.
23 − 7 16 = O	19 −12 7 = D	30 −16 14 = E	24 − 4 20 = E	28 −11 17 = I	15 −14 1 = R

6.	7.	8.	9.	10.	11.
26 −17 9 = G	27 −21 6 = V	18 −13 5 = Z	20 − 9 11 = T	29 − 3 26 = E	25 −22 3 = G

This person was the seventh president of the National Association of the Deaf (NAD), during which time a motion picture committee of the NAD was established to preserve and record sermons and presentations in American Sign Language. "Sign Language is God's noblest gift to the Deaf" is a translation of a line from his filmed presentation titled *Preservation of Sign Language*.

Answer on page 178.

CULTURE/LANGUAGE NOTES

Keeping Each Other Informed

If you were late for a history class, what would you do when you entered the classroom? Most people would quietly take their seat. That would be considered courteous behavior.

In a Sign Language class, however, that would not be appropriate. In addition to entering quietly you would be expected to take a moment to explain why you were late. You might say as briefly as possible, "Sorry for being late. I was talking to my friend Sarah." Sharing information is the norm in the Deaf community. Especially when there is a change in the routine or expectations, an explanation is warranted.

In the classroom you rehearsed ways of informing the teacher why you are late, why you are leaving early, and why you missed class. These are not to be viewed as giving excuses but rather viewed as a way of talk.

Why is this? Deaf people have formed a cohesive and mutually supportive community. As one would expect, this close-knit community encourages a greater sense of familiarity. This is evidenced in the kinds of information shared. Deaf people in everyday conversations share a great deal of information about their day-to-day lives talking about family, friends, what they've been doing, community news and events.

You will need to teach yourself to share more information about yourself when talking with Deaf people than you normally would with hearing people who are not close friends. This may seem like a small difference between hearing and Deaf cultures, but it is not. As you become more proficient in ASL, you will begin to appreciate how keeping others informed will affect how well you get to know Deaf people and how much of the Deaf community you will experience.

Begin by developing the following habits of informing others:

- If you are late or need to leave early, inform the other people and include an explanation.
- Let people know when you are leaving a group situation, not just one person or the host, but most people that you know.
- If you're leaving for a short while, tell someone where you're going and when you'll be back.

If you get up and leave a casual conversation, even if you were not directly involved, someone is likely to ask the group where you went. If you've told someone, that person will inform the group and the conversation will continue normally. In this way the expected level of information sharing is maintained.

End of Unit 6

KEY PHRASES

Ask what person did last Monday

Ask if person attended class this morning

Give reason for absence (doctor appointment)

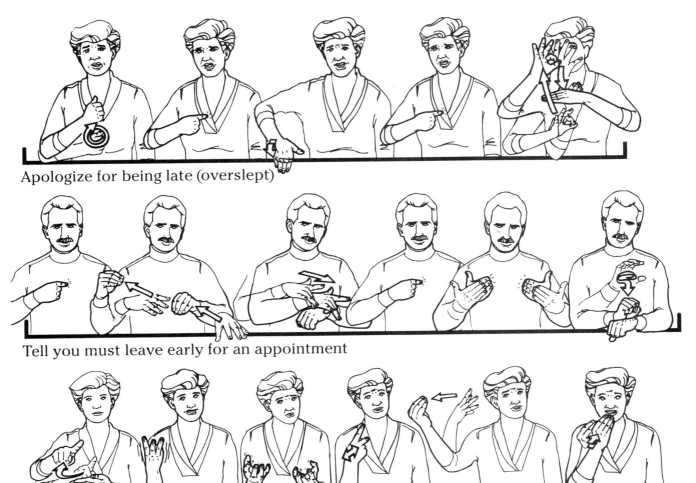

Apologize for being late (overslept)

Tell you must leave early for an appointment

Ask if person wants to go out to eat next Wednesday

Agree to suggestion

Decline (already made plans)

VOCABULARY REVIEW

DAYS OF THE WEEK

PARTS OF THE DAY

OTHER TIME SIGNS
February

Feb 16th

Feb 15th

Feb 17th

Feb 6 –12

Feb 20 – 26

ACTIVITIES AT HOME

ACTIVITIES OUTSIDE
OF THE HOME

PLACES

SPORTS AND
RECREATION

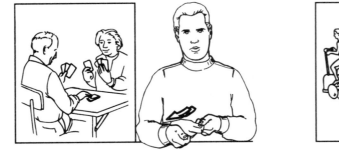 

APPOINTMENTS

**OPINIONS ABOUT
ACTIVITIES**

**REASONS FOR
BEING LATE**

NUMBERS
21 – 30

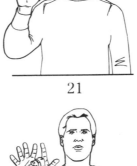

21

22

23

24

25

26

27

28

29

30

Units 1 – 6
Cumulative Review

LANGUAGE AND CULTURE

Getting Attention

On screen you will see several situations which focus on attention-getting behaviors. You are to determine whether or not the behavior in each scene is culturally appropriate. The correct answer will appear on screen. Scenes showing inappropriate behaviors will be immediately followed by a replay of the scene showing appropriate behaviors.

After you view the situations, read the summary of culturally appropriate behaviors that follows.

SUMMARY NOTES

Waving is the most common way to get attention. How big the wave is depends on how close you are to the person and how easily you can get his/her attention. If you're sitting across the table from someone, use a small wave. If someone is looking down (i.e., reading), wave small and low within the person's visual field. Waving increases in size as distance increases. Waving to someone across the room is acceptable if you can get the person's attention easily, and your wave is not outrageously demonstrative. If the distance is too great, you need a third person to get the other's attention.

Touching is another commonly used way to get attention. Touch is used especially when someone's back is to you, or when the person is involved in something (writing, reading, watching TV) so that your waving is not within his/her field of vision. Your touch should be gentle and firm. A few taps are acceptable-just one tap or too many taps are not acceptable. Tapping the shoulder or upper arm is most appropriate.

Negotiating a Signing Environment

On screen you will see several situations which focus on behaviors for negotiating a signing environment. You are to determine whether or not the behavior in each scene is culturally appropriate. Again, the correct answer will appear on screen and scenes showing inappropriate behaviors will be immediately followed by a replay of the scene showing appropriate behaviors.

After you view the situations, read the summary of culturally appropriate behaviors that follows.

70

SUMMARY NOTES

If two signers in conversation are blocking your way, i.e., standing in a doorway or stairwell, you can just walk through the conversation. You should add a slight head bow and the sign for "excuse me" as you go through. Don't stop and wait for them to acknowledge you or give you permission to go through. Passing through a conversation is not considered rude or inappropriate as long as the disruption is minimal.

If people are standing in one or more group conversations, you should go around or between groups, pressing people's backs or shoulders gently to let them know you need space to get through. Do not tap someone's shoulder and wait for acknowledgement unless you actually need people to move out of the way (i.e., if you're carrying a large object into the room).

If someone unknowingly blocks your view of a conversation, politely ask that person to move aside. Get his/her attention, then briefly explain the situation. Alternatively, you could ask the signer to move into a better view.

Conversation Strategies: Asking for Repetition

On screen you will see four sign phrases to use when you need clarification or repetition of something a signer said. The phrases should be used in the following situations:

Phrase 1: when you don't understand a sign
Phrase 2: if the signer is signing too fast for you
Phrase 3: if you missed a fingerspelled word
Phrase 4: if you were distracted and missed something

PAIR PRACTICE

Practice the behaviors you saw on screen by role playing the following situations with a partner:

Two-Person Role Play

Situation 1: A Deaf person is sitting at a desk facing a wall, typing a report. You need to ask him/her a question right away. Get his/her attention.

Situation 2: During a conversation, the person you're talking with moves in front of a window. The glare from the window is so bright that you can't see the person clearly. Ask the person to move.

Situation 3: You have just finished talking with your friend. As you walk away you notice something interesting happening outside the window. Get your friend's attention and tell him/her to look.

Situation 4: Your guest is leaving the room and you notice s/he forgot to take his/her pen. Run after the person, get his/her attention, and give the pen back.

You will need a third person to role play the next three situations:

Three-Person Role Play

Situation 1: You are conversing with someone sitting about ten feet away from you at a party. Someone inadvertently steps into your line of vision, blocking your view of the other person. Ask one or the other to move.

Situation 2: While at a ball game, you want to speak to a friend who is sitting two rows in front of you. Ask the person immediately in front of you to get your friend's attention.

Situation 3: You need to talk with your friend who is sitting two seats away from you. Lean over and get your friend's attention; if that doesn't work, ask the person next to you to assist.

Now practice the conversation strategies for getting clarification. Role play the following situations with a partner:

Two-Person Role Play: Asking for Repetition

Situation 1: Your friend uses a sign that you've never seen before.

Situation 2: Your friend is signing much too fast for you to follow the conversation.

Situation 3: Your friend just fingerspelled something, and you only got a few letters in the word.

Situation 4: While your friend was signing something to you, you were momentarily distracted by a sound. You realize your friend is waiting for your response, but you missed what s/he just said.

GRAMMAR PRACTICE

Sentence Types

Mary will sign 12 sentences. Indicate whether each sentence is a yes/no question, wh-word question, negative statement, or statement by circling the appropriate answer.

1. y/n   w h   neg   (statement)
2. y/n   (w h)   neg   statement
3. y/n   w h   neg   (statement)
4. (y/n)   w h   neg   statement
5. (y/n)   w h   neg   statement
6. y/n   (w h)   neg   statement

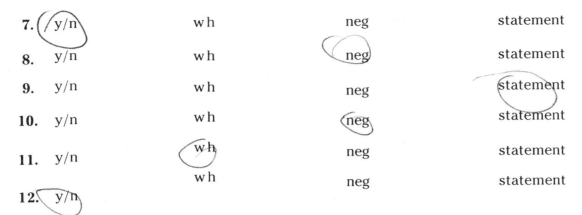

7. (y/n)   wh   neg   statement
8.   y/n   wh   (neg)   statement
9.   y/n   wh   neg   (statement)
10.   y/n   wh   (neg)   statement
11.   y/n   (wh)   neg   statement
        wh   neg   statement
12. (y/n)

Answers on page 179.

COMPREHENSION

Which Room Was It?

Cinnie tells a story about a Deaf couple on vacation who stop at a motel for the night.

How did the husband locate the right room? _honked the horn until all the lights went on except one_

Summary given on page 179.

CULTURE/LANGUAGE NOTES

Meeting Others

In Dialogue 1 on the classroom videotape, you saw a hearing student introduce herself to a Deaf person at a conference. The Deaf person asked the student key questions that have a definite cultural function. She asked where the student was learning ASL, whether or not her teacher was deaf, and the first and last name of the teacher.

This is a typical interaction strongly rooted in Deaf culture. The information exchanged explains how a person is connected to or affiliated with the Deaf community; in this case her affiliation is as a Sign Language student.

When Deaf people meet each other for the first time, the information exchanged is used to establish each other's community ties. In an introduction, the following information is shared: where they are from; which residential school they attended, including the year they entered and the year they graduated; whether they attended Gallaudet University; if yes, what class (i.e., Class of 1975).

Based on this information, they will begin to talk about people they might know in common and share personal information. In the Deaf community, almost everyone's connection can be established either directly or indirectly. How is this? Most deaf children attend residential schools. They live at these schools throughout the school year, from kindergarten through high school. Most students view the school as their home, and their fellow students as part of their extended family. After completing school, Deaf people continue to strengthen their social bonds by participating in various Deaf community activities, i.e., athletic tournaments, clubs, churches, picnics, and other social events. Former classmates, co-workers, friends, and acquaintances drive for miles to attend these events, maintaining contact with each other and sharing news about themselves, mutual friends, and the community at large.

Deaf people you meet for the first time will be interested in finding out about your connection to the Deaf community. When introducing yourself, prepare to share the following information:

- your first and last name
- whether you are deaf, hard of hearing, or hearing
- who is teaching you the language and culture
- where you are studying
- why you are learning the language

Name Signs

When a deaf child first enters residential school, a dorm counselor will often assign a name sign using the first letter of the child's name. Two examples are:

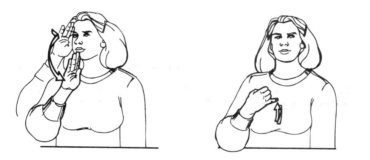

In the cases where children have Deaf parents, name signs are given at birth. Not everyone has a name sign. Three- and four-letter names are often just fingerspelled.

Name signs are used for identifying and referring to people both present and not present. Name signs are not used in direct address, that is, when you're signing to Mary you would not use her name sign to say "I don't think so, Mary."

There are two kinds of name signs: arbitrary and descriptive. The examples above are arbitrary: they use the first letter of the person's name, and their location and movement are governed by linguistic rules. Descriptive name signs are derived from distinctive physical features, i.e., a description of someone's hairstyle, a mole on the cheek, cleft chin. These are similar to descriptions used in identifying people. Descriptive name signs are often given by peers (i.e., other children in residential school) and are almost always replaced in adulthood by an arbitrary name sign.

Descriptive name signs are sometimes given to hearing Sign Language students for use in the classroom. These differ from the descriptive name signs given by deaf peers in that they often use the first letter of the student's name in conjunction with some descriptive feature. These should not be used as a way of identifying oneself outside of class. It is not until hearing people are involved in the community, either through work or social relationships, that an arbitrary name sign may be given. Name signs should be given by a Deaf person; hearing people should not invent their own name signs. Even if you have an arbitrary name sign, when asked your name, you must first spell your full name.

How Do Deaf People . . . ?

Know when a baby is crying or the phone is ringing? How do deaf people know when there's someone at the door, or if a smoke detector is going off? For all of these sounds, there are flashing-light signalling devices. You saw Esther, the babysitter, explain or use these devices in Dialogue 3 of the Cumulative Review classroom videotape. She explains that when the baby cries, a light flashes and she knows to check on the baby. You also saw the light flash when the telephone rang. Doorbells and smoke detectors can be attached to similar devices. The lights flash in a distinctive rhythm so the deaf person knows what to respond to.

Wake up in the morning? For the people who don't wake up on their own, there are special alarm clocks attached to either a flashing light or a bed vibrator that is activated when the alarm goes off.

Understand TV? Many television shows are captioned. To be able to see these captions on screen, deaf people must have a device called a "decoder" attached to the TV. Captions appear like subtitles on the bottom of the screen so that deaf people can read what's being said. These captions also mention sounds that are off-screen, such as applause or a telephone ringing.

Talk on the phone? There is a special telecommunication device that enables deaf people to use the telephone. In the Deaf community this device is called a TTY (short for teletypewriter), while hearing businesses use the term TDD (Telecommunication Device for the Deaf). When the phone rings, the deaf person places the receiver on a coupler attached to the TTY device. The device has a small keyboard and the conversation takes place by typing back and forth.

In order for a conversation to take place, there must be a TTY at both ends. However, some community agencies or businesses provide relay services to mediate communication between TTY and voice calls. A relay-service operator types what the hearing person says, and then reads aloud what the deaf person types. Ask your teacher for your local relay service phone numbers and write them in below.

voice: _____

TTY: _____

End of Cumulative Review: Units 1 - 6

KEY PHRASES

Introduce someone

Ask another person to get someone's attention

Ask to repeat

Ask to slow down

Ask what was said

Ask to repeat fingerspelling

Tell you don't understand

Unit 7
Giving Directions

LANGUAGE IN ACTION

Conversation 1

Kim (A), a Sign Language student, approaches Cinnie (B) in the stairway of a college building to ask directions to the soda machine.

    A: explain problem with soda machine, ask if B knows where another soda machine is
    B: tell where you think one is (on another floor), ask if A knows where
    A: respond negatively
    B: check if A knows where the elevator is
    A: confirm
    B: give directions from there
    A: repeat directions to confirm
    B: confirm
    A: express thanks
    A and B: say goodbye

Conversation 2

Ella (B) and Ken (C) are sitting outdoors, chatting over lunch. Ben (A) joins them and asks Ella where he can buy a sandwich.

    A, B and C: greet each other
    A: (to B) say that you're hungry, explain you forgot to bring a sandwich, ask where B got her sandwich
    B: explain that you brought it from home
    A: respond, **ask where you can buy** one
    B: point to location
    A: ask if it's near the bookstore
    B: correct, **give more specific location**, check with C to confirm
    C: (to A) **give more specific information**
    A: respond, ask if you can leave your jacket, give reason; **say that you will be back**
    B and C: agree
    A: express thanks (leave)
    B and C: (continue conversation)

Key phrases that express target language functions are highlighted. Replay the videotape until you can follow the conversations without the aid of the cues. Then rehearse both conversations, especially the key phrases.

CONVERSATION PRACTICE

To practice the key phrases in a new context, find a partner and role play the following situations:

Situation 1: A new student in class asks you how to get to the nearest bus stop. (Other possible locations: gym, park, grocery store, swimming pool, etc.)

Situation 2: Approach an information desk in a large office complex and ask where a certain room or office is located.

GRAMMAR NOTES

Cardinal and Ordinal Numbers

By now you have learned the basic handshapes for cardinal (or counting) numbers. While the handshapes remain the same, different movements and locations are used for different kinds of numbers, i.e., age numbers, ordinal numbers, money numbers. In this unit, we focus on ordinal numbers.

Ordinal numbers indicate order in a series. These numbers have the following forms:

"first" to "ninth"	Made with a twist of the wrist towards the body, with the hand in a more horizontal position than the position for cardinal numbers.
"tenth" and up	Usually made with the same form as cardinal numbers, but adding fingerspelled "th" at the end. Sometimes just the number is used if the context is clear.

Ordinal Numbers

On screen, Ken will model ordinal numbers "first" to "tenth." Replay the tape and practice signing the numbers.

GRAMMAR NOTES

Giving Directions

To give directions to a place in a building, go from general to specific. For example, to give directions to the teacher's office:

1) Give the general location: "upstairs, on the fourth floor"
2) Identify a starting point on that floor: "as you leave the elevator. . ."
3) Give specific directions from the starting point: "turn left, pass the drinking fountain, and it's the second door on your right"

To give directions to someone familiar with the building, use a **common reference point** (i.e., that you and the listener both know). For example, for the same teacher's office:

1) Establish a common reference point: "you know the drinking fountain on the fourth floor?"
2) Give specific directions to the desired location: "pass the drinking fountain, and it's the second door on the right"

Use the skills described in "Spatial Agreement" in Unit 3, i.e., eye gaze/location agreement and non-manual behaviors showing relative distance, so that your listener can visualize the route or location you describe.

Mary will model giving directions in the next videotaped activity.

GRAMMAR PRACTICE

Giving Directions

Ben will ask Mary where he can find various things in the building illustrated below.
Find #1 on the illustration, then watch Mary give directions to that location. Then do the same for #2 and #3.

Giving Directions Using a Common Reference

Again, Ben will ask Mary where he can find various things in the building. Watch how she signs directions to locations marked #4, #5 and #6 in the illustration. Notice how she establishes a common reference point.

Rewind the tape to the beginning of this activity. After Ben signs each question, stop the tape and give directions. Then compare your directions with Mary's.

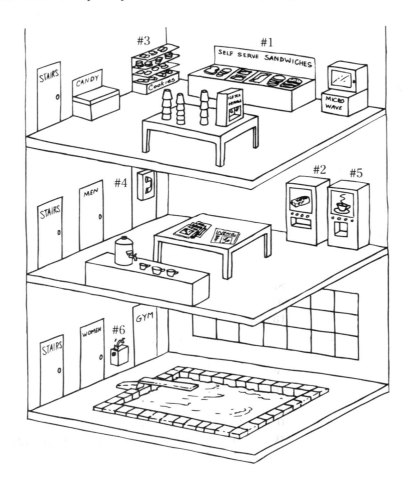

PAIR PRACTICE

Practice 1. Find a partner and go to a building with several floors. Divide the floors up between yourselves; for example, you go to the first and second floors while your partner goes to the third and fourth floors. Take a short tour of your floors to familiarize yourself with the locations of various places. Then give your partner a list of places on those floors that s/he could ask about.

Ask each other where the things or places on your lists are located. Practice giving directions, going from general to specific as described in the Grammar Note above.

Practice 2. Go to a location that you and your partner are familiar with. Collect several things, such as a book, jacket, candy bar, and put them in other rooms. Your partner is to ask where each thing is located. Establish a common reference point as you give directions to the location of each object.

COMPREHENSION

Fingerspelling, Part 3

Five signers will sign a total of 12 sentences with one fingerspelled word in each. You are to write down the word that is spelled. You don't need to write the whole sentence.

1. ice
2. TV
3. date
4. cake
5. oil
6. fun

7. high school
8. man apt
9. 7-up
10. TTY
11. van
12. cake

Answers on page 179.

PAIR PRACTICE

Sign sentences to your partner, using one fingerspelled word in each sentence (fingerspell words and abbreviated forms from both your list above and the list below). Have your partner repeat the fingerspelled word you used.

bus	car	dept (department)	ID (identification)
toy	bag	ref (refrigerator)	gas
OK	job	OT (overtime)	VCR

The Candy Bar

Ben tells a story about a person waiting in an airport lounge for a delayed flight. Write a summary of the story.

Summary given on page 179.

man went to air port - waited in line to buy ticket. His flight is delayed. He bought newspaper, candy, coffee. He found a seat & started reading. Man next to him ate his candy bar. He took bite himself. other man ate the rest. Man very angry but boarded plane, got on plane & sat. Plane took off & he found a candy bar but it was his candy.

CULTURE/LANGUAGE NOTES

Cross-Cultural Communication

Ninety percent of all deaf children have hearing parents. A small percentage of these parents learn Sign Language. Consequently, Deaf people at a very early age develop strategies for communicating with people who do not sign. Some of the the most common strategies are described below:

Pen and paper are used for seeking information, conducting business (i.e., getting directions, placing orders), or having conversations. This is the most common strategy for cross-cultural communication.

Gesturing is usually used with people seen regularly and in situations where the interaction is predictable. This form of communication is used to manage limited social contact with people like the regular waitress at the local coffee shop, relatives, co-workers, neighbors. If the interaction continues, other strategies such as pen and paper are usually used.

Lipreading and speech are among the least preferred strategies for most Deaf people. Approximately thirty percent of spoken English can be understood by lipreading, which leaves the Deaf person in an untenable position. This percentage can increase if the hearing person or the subject is familiar, or if the content is predictable (i.e., "how are you?" in a greeting). Lipreading leaves considerable room for misunderstanding, and because of this, it is held to a minimum. The use of speech varies with each individual. Few Deaf people feel comfortable using speech with strangers.

Adapting signs to others (or modifying Sign Language for communicative purposes) is used with hearing people with varying degrees of signing ability. Deaf people will vary their signs to match the language skills of the other person. This might mean the inclusion of more fingerspelled words, more mouthing of words, gesturing, simple sentences, slower pace, more English-like word order. The goal is to communicate, so Deaf people will use whatever combination of methods is most effective. This is similar to what you would do with a person who is obviously foreign born and not fluent in the English language.

Using a third person to interpret is another strategy to help make conversations between Deaf and hearing persons flow more smoothly. The third person would sign what was said and voice what was signed. In many situations such as medical, legal, educational and professional, Deaf people prefer to use certified Sign Language interpreters who not only know the language fluently, but are sensitive to Deaf and hearing cultures as well.

Strategies for Sign Language students:
- Let the Deaf person know that you can sign.
- Let the Deaf person set the communication pattern to be used.
- Avoid talking (using voice) in the presence of a Deaf person without relaying the information in signs. It is considered rude not to keep the Deaf person informed.
- If you see other people signing, avoid watching their conversation unless you intend to introduce yourself.

End of Unit 7

KEY PHRASES

Explain need (hungry), ask where restaurant is

Tell where (across from the gym)

Explain problem (locked bathroom), ask where's another

82

VOCABULARY REVIEW

PLACES

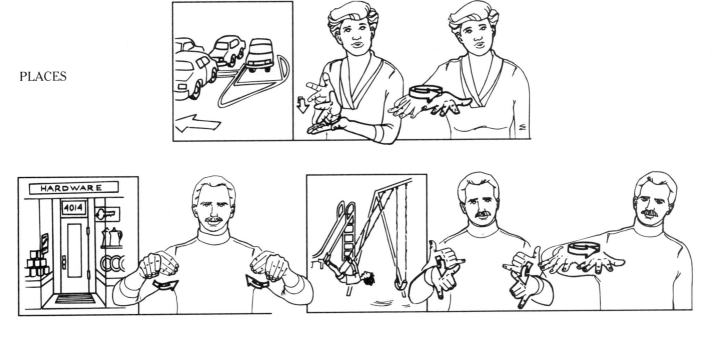

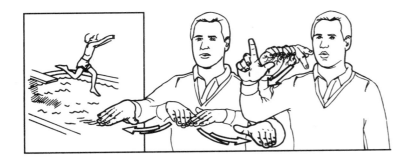

WITHIN THE
BUILDING

INDICATING LOCATIONS

PROBLEMS

SNACKS

EXPRESS NEEDS

 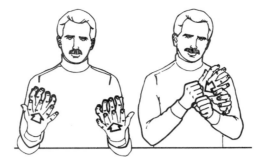 

SIZES OF DRINKS

WITH/WITHOUT

EXPRESSING DEGREES OF CERTAINTY

```
├──────────┼──────────┤
Certain   Somewhat    Uncertain
          uncertain
```

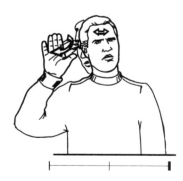
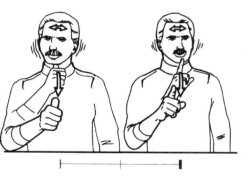

Unit 8
Describing Others

LANGUAGE IN ACTION

Conversation 1

Flo (A) is walking her dog in a park when she runs into Mary (B).

A: (walking dog)
B: greet B with surprise
A: greet A with surprise, ask if she lives here
B: reply affirmatively, explain that you brought kids here to play
A: express surprise, ask if B has children
B: explain they're your husband's children from his first marriage
A: ask where the kids are on the playground
B: identify daughter
A: give additional descriptions to confirm
B: confirm
B: identify son
A: give additional descriptions to confirm
B: confirm
A: make comment, ask if kids are deaf
B: tell that one is deaf, and one is hearing
A: explain that you live nearby, that you could come back (dog pulls leash) and that the dog wants to go
A and B: say goodbye

Conversation 2

Brian (A), the father of a young boy, approaches the person (B) working at the lost and found office at a public pool.

A and B: greet each other
A: explain that your son lost two pieces of clothing, request help
B: ask for description
A: describe items
B: repeat descriptions to make sure
A: confirm
B: tell that you'll go look for them (leave and return with items), ask if first item is correct
A: (check jacket), **confirm**
B: (hand over second item)
A: (check shorts) **correct description** for shorts
B: repeat correct description (go look again and return), **express regret**
A: complain about son losing things, express thanks
B: say goodbye

Key phrases that express target language functions are highlighted. Replay the videotape until you can follow the conversations without the aid of the cues. Then rehearse both conversations, especially the key phrases.

CONVERSATION PRACTICE

To practice the key phrases in a new context, find a partner and role play the situations below:

Situation 1: You are at a convention. You need to get a message to a person waiting in the lobby that you will be delayed 30 minutes. Your friend is willing to relay the message but doesn't know what the person looks like. (Possible person: your sister, your spouse, your parent, your daughter or son, your aunt or uncle, your girlfriend or boyfriend.)

Situation 2: People at your office are pooling money to buy a gift for a co-worker. You're in charge of buying the gift. Unsure of the person's taste in clothes, you consult others.

GRAMMAR NOTES

Identifying Others

There are certain norms to follow for identifying and describing people:

- Point out the person and describe his/her most noticeable or distinguishing characteristics (see list below for what to describe).
- Make sure your listener understands who you're talking about - do not go on until you get **confirmation** that s/he knows who you mean. Identifying people is an **interactive** process.

The way you identify someone varies slightly depending on whether the person is present and within sight or not present.

If you want to identify someone who is **present and within sight**, begin your sentence with raised eyebrows and this sign:

Then point to the person and describe him/her, keeping your eyebrows raised throughout the description. Descriptions of people tend to follow a particular order. Gender is always mentioned first; then, in general:

- height
- body type
- color of hair
- hairstyle

Other characteristics are mentioned right after gender if they distinguish the person from others in that situation (i.e., race, distinctive facial features, eyeglasses, jewelry, clothing, and whether s/he is sitting, standing, or signing).

When your listener nods or gives confirming descriptions of the person you identified, proceed with comments or questions about that person.

If you want to identify someone who is **not present**, begin your sentence with raised eyebrows and this sign:

Then go on to describe the person in the same general order, adding information about where the listener might have seen the person. If the listener indicates that s/he doesn't know who you mean, continue your description with occupation, personal qualities, habits, and the person's relationship to other people the listener knows. When the listener indicates (with a nod or confirming question) that s/he recognizes the person you identified, continue with your comments or question.

In the next activity, Ben will model how to identify people present in the room, and Mary will model how to confirm or acknowledge that she knows who he means.

GRAMMAR PRACTICE

Identifying Others

On screen Ben and Mary will first demonstrate how to identify and acknowledge others in the room. This is followed by four dialogues showing different ways of identifying people. Pay particular attention to how the listener confirms which person the speaker is referring to; notice that the speaker does not proceed until the listener confirms the right person.

Dialogue 1

Ben: **identify** person (by gender, color and style of hair, facial feature)

Mary: **confirm** (by adding information about clothing)

Ben: **confirm** that it's the right person, then ask question

Mary: give information

Ben: respond

Dialogue 2

Mary: **identify** person (by gender and distinctive facial feature)

Ben: **confirm** (by adding information about body type)

Mary: **confirm** that it's the right person, give information

Ben: respond

Dialogue 3

Mary: **identify** person (by gender, height, and hairstyle)

Ben: **confirm** (by adding information about body type)

Mary: **correct** (by adding information about location of person

Ben: **acknowledge**, **confirm** (by adding description of clothing)

Mary: **confirm**, give information

Ben: respond

Dialogue 4

Ben: **identify** person (by gender, eyeglasses, location)

Mary: **confirm** (by describing hairstyle)

Ben: **correct** (by emphasizing eyeglasses)

Mary: **acknowledge**

Ben: ask information

Mary: give information

Ben: comment

Mary: agree

PAIR PRACTICE

Find a partner and practice identifying others who are present and within sight. Follow the cued dialogues above to practice different ways of identifying people and different sequences of acknowledging the person. (Possible environments: lobby of a hotel, beach, railroad station, coffee shop.)

Numbers: Multiples of 10 and 11

Cinnie will model numbers in multiples of 10 (from 20 to 100), and then Brian will model numbers in multiples of 11 (from 11 to 99). Replay the tape and practice signing the numbers.

COMPREHENSION

Personal Data

Ben will give you personal information about each of the people pictured below. Write the information he gives under the appropriate picture. Stop the tape after each sentence to give yourself time to write.

Answers on page 180.

PAIR PRACTICE

Give additional information to your partner about each person pictured above. First identify the person, then wait until your partner acknowledges the right person before you give the information. Each of you should write down the information given.

Missing Number

Different signers will give you sequences of numbers (multiples of 5, 10 and 11). Figure out the number missing from each sequence. Write down only the number that's missing.

Example: _____20_____   3. _____

    1. _____   4. _____

    2. _____   5. _____

Answers given on page 180.

End of Unit 8

KEY PHRASES

Identify person

Ask for confirmation

Confirm, ask who

Describe clothing

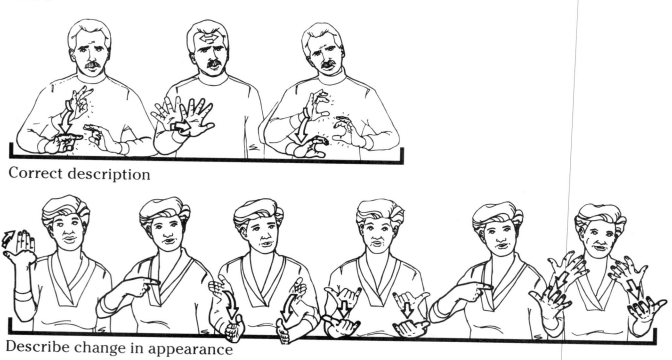

Correct description

Describe change in appearance

VOCABULARY REVIEW

ETHNICITY

DESCRIBE HAIR

Hair lengths

Hair types

DESCRIBE FACES

Shape of faces

Facial hair

Facial features

DESCRIBE HEIGHTS

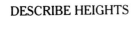 

99

DESCRIBE
BODY TYPES

CLOTHING

STYLES OF CLOTHING

PATTERNS
ON CLOTHES

ACCESSORIES

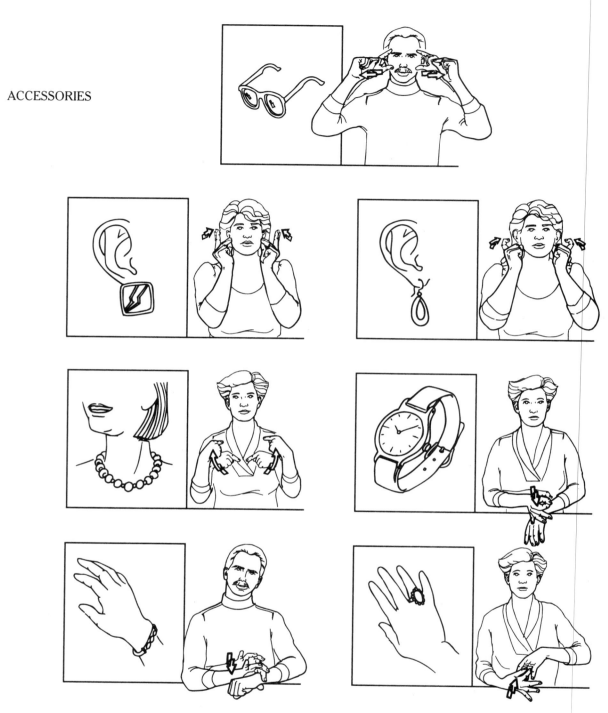

NUMBERS

Multiples of 10 and 11

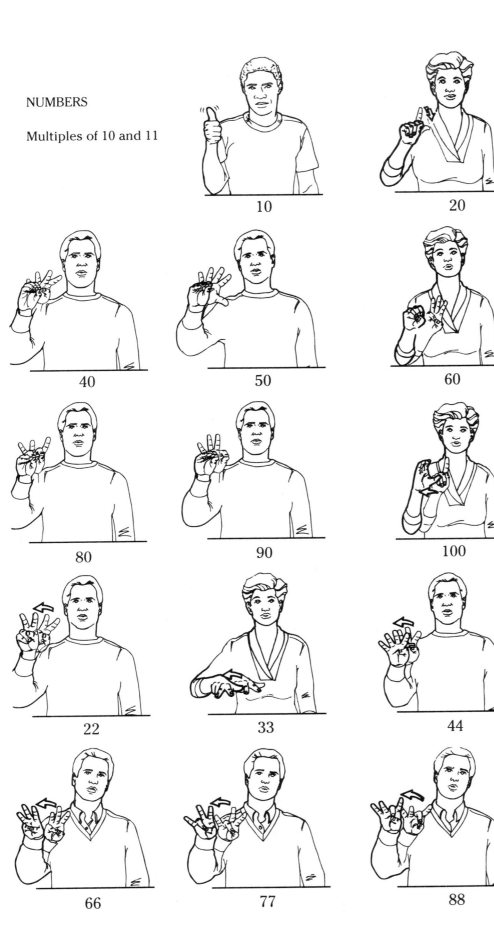

10   20   30

40   50   60   70

80   90   100   11

22   33   44   55

66   77   88   99

Unit 9
Making Requests

LANGUAGE IN ACTION

Conversation 1

Two friends are getting ready for a party. Ben (A) is cooking something in the kitchen when Ken (B) arrives with a bag of groceries.

B: make comment
A: request help
B: agree, ask what you can do
A: request that he bring over a neighbor's folding table
B: accept, ask where it is
A: tell where to go get it
B: identify neighbor to confirm
A: confirm
B: respond, ask where to put it
A: tell where
B: respond, tell that you are going to get it now
A: (remember something), ask another favor
B: respond, offer more help
A: express thanks

Conversation 2

Cinnie (A) is visiting Ella (B). Cinnie is getting ready to leave. She remembers that Ella has to submit a report for class, so she asks her about it.

A: ask if B has completed the report
B: reply negatively, explain why
A: offer assistance (babysitting)
B: accept offer
A: ask when a good time would be
B: explain that the report is due Monday, suggest the Saturday before
A: agree
B: express thanks
A: accept, leavetaking (stand up and nearly trip over toy)
B: apologize
A: offer to help clean up
B: decline, tell why
A: agree
A and B: say goodbye

Key phrases that express target language functions are highlighted. Replay the videotape until you can follow the conversations without the aid of the cues. Then rehearse both conversations, especially the key phrases.

CONVERSATION PRACTICE

To practice the key phrases in a new context, find a partner and role play the situations below:

Situation 1: Your partner is complaining about something. Offer assistance. (Possible complaints: house is a mess, TV is on the blink, faucet is leaking, need a hair cut, grass in yard is overgrown, basketball hoop fell down, etc.)

Situation 2: Your friend plans to go to the store and asks you if there's anything you need. Possible needs:

- milk (specify size)
- toothpaste (specify tube or pump)
- dog food (specify brand and size)
- laundry detergent (specify size and describe the box)

GRAMMAR NOTES

Money Numbers

Money numbers, like ordinal numbers described in Unit 7, have their own distinctive forms. In this unit we focus on the numbers expressing how many cents.

The form for money numbers under a dollar is a combination of the sign "cent" (index finger moving out from the forehead) and the number. Some signers may fingerspell "cents" after the number is signed, i.e., 77 cents, 39 cents.

The form for "1 dollar" is similar to the ordinal number "first." "1 dollar" can be made with a slightly bigger twist of the wrist and with a wider arc than the ordinal number. You may have to rely on context to distinguish whether it's "first" or "1 dollar" that's being signed.

You will see examples of money numbers in the next videotaped segment.

GRAMMAR PRACTICE

Money Numbers

Mary will model money numbers for 1, 5, 10, 15, 20, and 25 cents. She will then model money numbers in tens from 60 to 90 cents, and in tens from 55 to 95 cents. Finally, she will model the sign for 1 dollar.

Notice where her palm faces for each number sign. Replay the tape and imitate each sign.

GRAMMAR NOTES

Verb Types

There are three types of verbs in ASL: plain, inflecting, and spatial.*

Plain verbs require the signer to specify the subject and object. Consider the verbs below. If you use them in a sentence, you have to explicitly mention who is doing what with whom; the verbs themselves do not convey that information.

Inflecting verbs, unlike plain verbs, allow the signer to indicate the subject and object by changing the direction of movement of the sign. Consider the first two signs below: the signs start at the subject and end at the object. The verb can also be inflected to indicate the number of subjects and/or objects - see the third illustration below.

(I to you) (s/he to me) (I to all of you)

Spatial verbs, like inflecting verbs, allow the signer to change the direction of movement of the sign to indicate location (i.e., from here to there). Like plain verbs, however, the subject and object must be specified. For example:

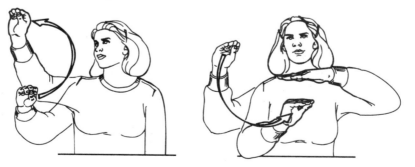

*This breakdown of verb types is from Carol Padden, "Interaction of Morphology and Syntax in American Sign Language " unpublished doctoral dissertation, 1983, University of California, San Diego.

GRAMMAR PRACTICE

Verb Types: Skit 1, 2, 3

On screen you will observe three different skits. Each skit will be followed by a narrator summarizing what happened. In each narrative, observe how spatial and inflecting verbs are used. Mary narrates Skit 1 using spatial verbs; Cinnie and Ben narrate Skits 2 and 3 using inflecting verbs.

After you have seen all the skits and narratives, replay each skit and narrate what happened. Compare your narrative with the one that follows on screen.

COMPREHENSION

Give and Take

Ella will sign five accounts of three people giving and taking money. She will ask a question at the end of each account about how much money one person has. Stop the tape and write your answers below.

	Who?	How Much?
1.	Sally	0
2.	Jane	35¢
3.	Bob	none
4.	Bob	30¢
5.	Sally	35¢

Answers on page 180.

Making Requests

On screen five signers will sign narratives about making requests. Write the letter that appears on screen next to the picture that matches the narrative. If you need more time, stop the tape after each narrative.

B ___   A ___

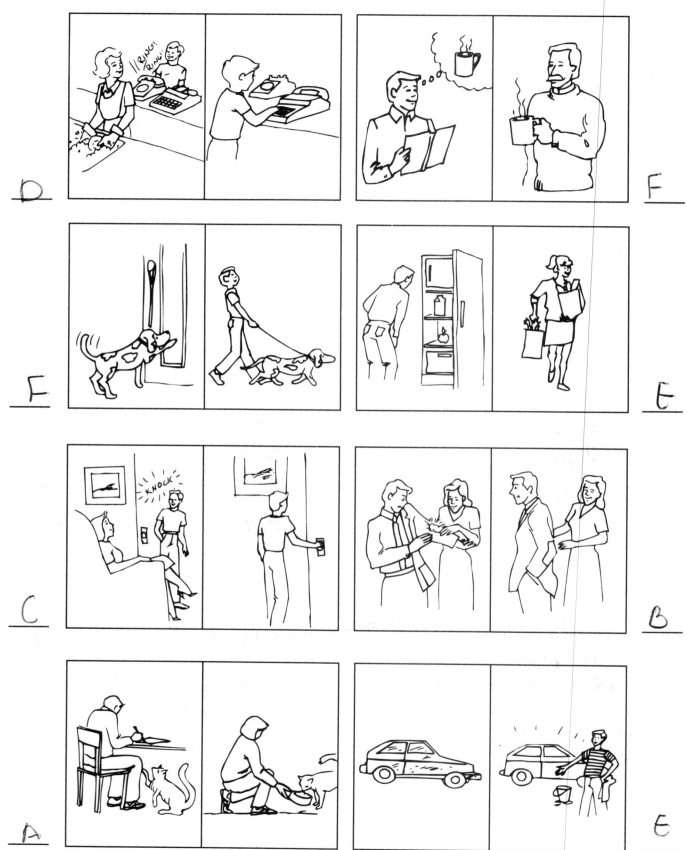

Answers on page 181.

PAIR PRACTICE

Practice making requests by asking your partner to get the objects pictured on the following page. First, decide which of you will assign locations for the numbered objects, and which of you will assign locations for the lettered objects. Write the numbers (or letters) of the objects in different locations in the kitchen pictured below. When done, follow the dialogue format below, and have your partner mark the letter or number of the object in the location specified. Take turns being Signer A.

> **A:** give reason, request that B get an object from the kitchen
> **B:** agree, ask where
> **A:** identify location, tell where object is in relation to that location
> **B:** (mark corresponding location in your picture)

Afterwards, compare pictures to check that you each marked the correct location for each object.

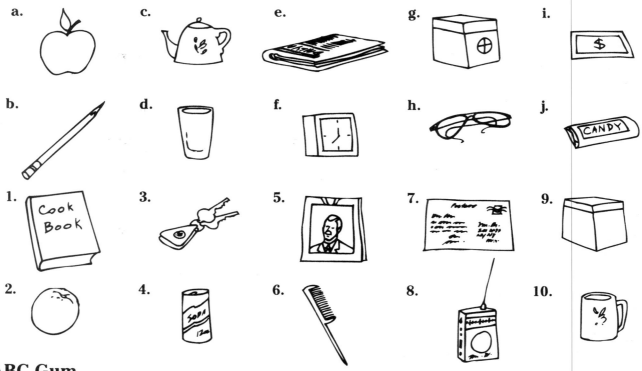

ABC Gum

Ella tells a story about a boy who is not supposed to have gum. One day while he's chewing gum his mother calls him. He sticks the gum on the bench, then goes off. The story goes on to tell what happened to the gum.

Write a summary of the story. Include the different places the gum ended up, and how each person found it.

Summary given on page 182.

End of Unit 9

Man sat on bench reading. Gum stuck on his pants. threw it on sidewalk. Woman was walking and stepped on it. She threw it at a tree and it stuck. Girl standing against tree and a boy put his hand on it and got stuck. He put it on the bench and the boy came back. He found the gum and put it back in his mouth and blew bubbles

KEY PHRASES

Make request (to close window)

Make request (to borrow a dollar)

Agree to request

Agree to request

Agree to request for help

Offer assistance (to paint)

Offer assistance (to assemble)

Accept assistance   Accept assistance

Decline assistance (almost done)

Decline assistance (will do it yourself)

VOCABULARY REVIEW

INFLECTING VERBS

SPATIAL VERBS

 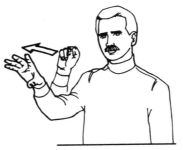

OBJECTS AROUND
THE ROOM

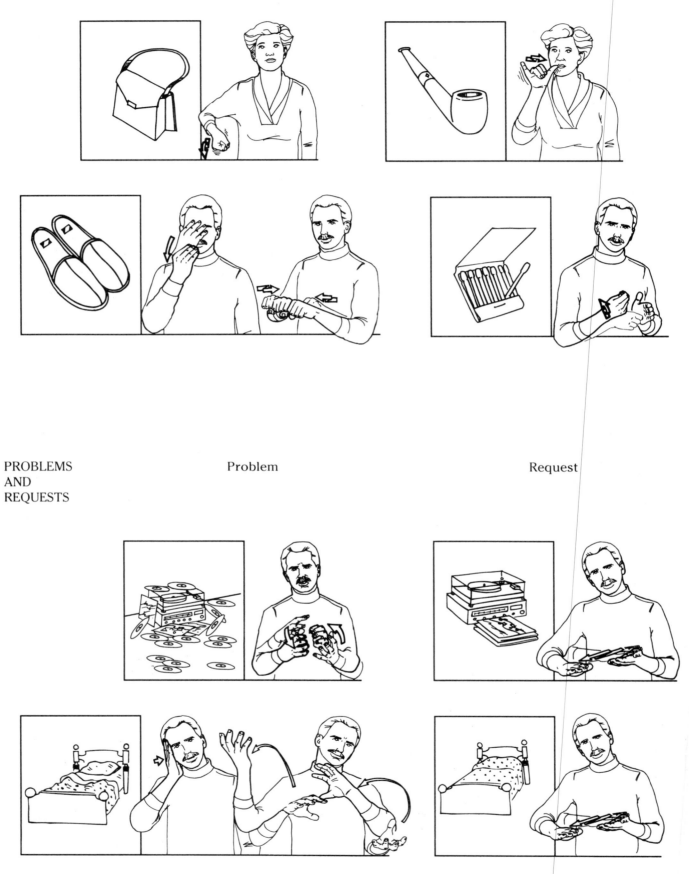

PROBLEMS
AND
REQUESTS

Problem

Request

Problem   Request

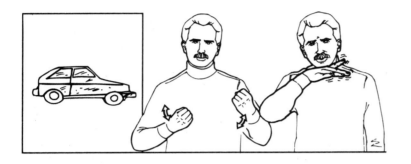

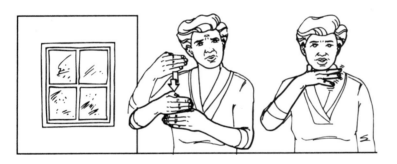

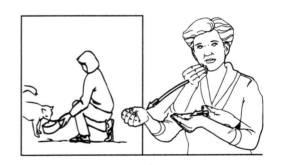

Problem   Request

Problem   Request

 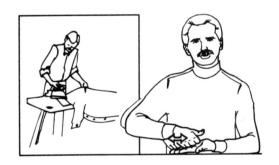

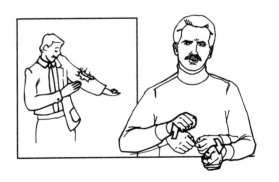 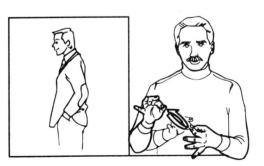

Problem   Request

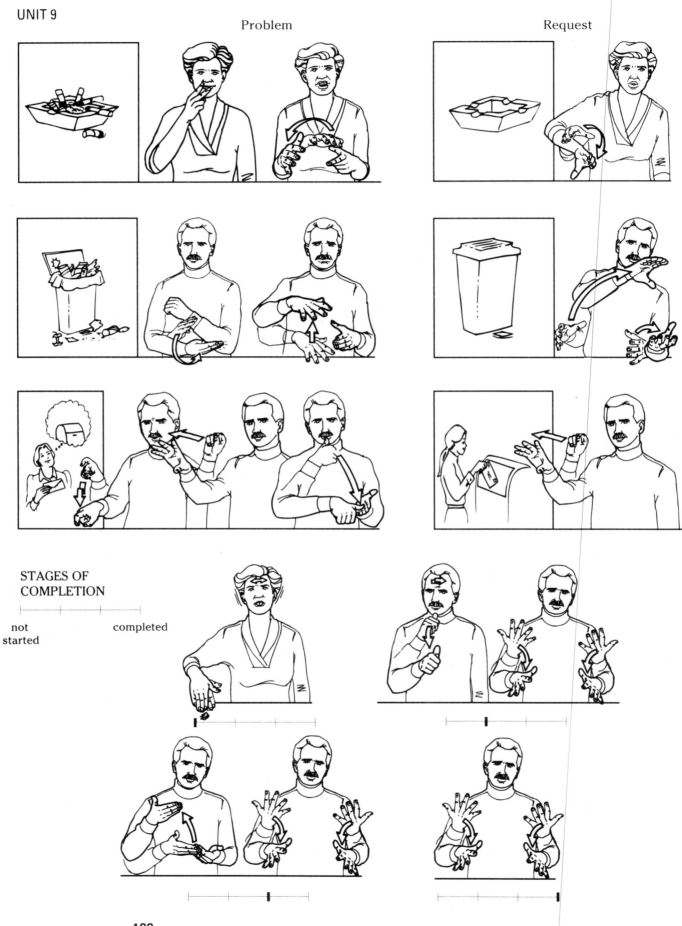

STAGES OF
COMPLETION

not   completed
started

MONEY NUMBERS

1¢

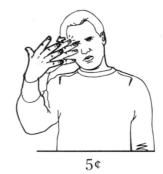

5¢

10¢

15¢

20¢

25¢

50¢

55¢

60¢

65¢

70¢

75¢

80¢

85¢

90¢

95¢

$1.00

Unit 10
Talking About Family and Occupations

LANGUAGE IN ACTION

Conversation 1

Brian (B) missed work last Friday. On Monday, Mary (A) asks Brian about his absence.

A: greet B, ask about absence
B: give explanation (parents' wedding anniversary)
A: ask how long parents have been married
B: tell how long
A: respond, ask how many brothers and sisters B has
B: tell how many, **tell where you rank among siblings**
A: ask where siblings live
B: tell where each one lives
A: comment, **ask if siblings are close to each other**
B: reply
A: respond

Conversation 2

Flo (A), an employer, is interviewing Ben (B), a job applicant.

A: ask if B is working right now
B: reply affirmatively and **tell where**
A: ask about tasks performed
B: explain tasks
A: ask if B likes his present job
B: reply affirmatively
A: ask if B gets along with others at work
B: reply affirmatively

Key phrases that express target language functions are highlighted. Replay the videotape until you can follow the conversations without the aid of the cues. Then rehearse both conversations, especially the key phrases.

CONVERSATION PRACTICE

To practice the key phrases in a new context, find a partner and role play the situations below:

Situation 1: You are at the 20-year reunion of your high school class. You would like to tell a former classmate about what you've been doing all these years. Tell about your spouse/relationship and children. Tell how long you've been in the relationship and how old each child is.

Situation 2: You are interviewing people to find participants for Career Day at a local high school. Ask your partner to explain his/her job.

GRAMMAR NOTES

Personal and Possessive Pronouns

Personal pronouns (I, you, s/he) are signed with the index finger. Possessive pronouns (my, your, his/her) are signed with the B-handshape (with thumb extended).

Pronouns	English	ASL
personal:	I/me	index finger points to yourself
	you	index finger points to the person you are talking to
	he/she/it him/her	index finger points to the person (if present) or to space designating that person*
possessive:	my/mine	pat your chest with B-hand
	your/yours	B-hand faces the person(s) you are talking to
	his/her/its	B-hand faces the third person (if present) or to space designating that person*

Age Numbers

Forming Age Numbers. The sign form for **age numbers** is a combination of the sign indicating age and the number itself. To indicate age, the index finger contacts the chin (the contraction of the sign for "old") and is followed by the number. There is a variation where the sign for "old" in its original form is used in conjunction with the number. On videotape you will see the contracted form for showing age numbers. Pay attention to which direction Cinnie's palm is facing as she signs the numbers.

Ranking by Age. When talking about three or more children or siblings in a family, you would usually **rank each child by age** on your non-dominant hand. The oldest is represented by the thumb or index finger, depending on the number. You can continue to give additional information by simply pointing to the finger representing that family member.

Observe how this is done in the "Talking About Children" segment on screen.

*If you are talking about a person who is not present in the room, first indicate who and designate a space to your right or left to represent that person. Then every time you point to that designated space, it functions like "he" or "she." You should continue using the same point of reference as long as you are talking about that person.

GRAMMAR PRACTICE

Age Numbers

Cinnie will model age numbers for 1 to 20 years old. Replay the tape and practice signing the numbers.

Talking About Children

You will see four signers talk about their children. Observe when and how the signers use ranking to talk about children.

Signer #1: has one child
Signer #2: has two children   (contrastive structure used)
Signer #3: has three children   (ranking used)
Signer #4: has six children   (ranking used)

Notice how the signer talks about the sixth child in the family. He signs the ordinal number sixth with his non-dominant hand and points to it with his other hand.

Watch Signer #4 again and write down the information given about each of the six children.

_____

_____

_____

_____

_____

_____

Answers on page 182.

COMPREHENSION

A Show of Hands

Two contestants appear on the game show, "A Show of Hands: Deaf Trivia." The host of the show begins by interviewing each contestant.

Watch the whole segment, then go back and watch it again to answer the following questions:

1. What personal information did each contestant give?

Contestant 1: _____

_____

_____

Contestant 2: _____

_____

_____

2. What was the first question asked?

_____

3. What answers did Carol (Cinnie) give?

_____

4. What was the second question asked?

_____

5. What answers did Janie (Mary) give?

_____

6. Which answer was incorrect and why?

_____

7. What correct answer did Carol (Cinnie) give instead?

_____

Answers on page 182.

Fingerspelling, Part 4

In each segment you will see three fingerspelled words. All three words have a common two- or three-letter combination. Write down the common letter combination from the list below. The activity begins with an example.

OY	PH	CH	GL	WI	NN
BR	NT	TT	GHT	ING	EE

Example __*CH*__

1. _____   **5**. _____

2. _____   **6**. _____

3. _____   **7**. _____

4. _____   **8**. _____

Answer on page 182.

End of Unit 10

KEY PHRASES

Ask how old person is

Ask how old when person first flew

Ask how old person started to read

Tell when you did it (34 years old)

Tell you have never done it

Ask where person ranks among children

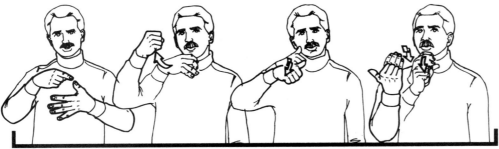

Tell age of oldest child (15 years old)

Ask how long the two of them have been married

Ask how long person worked for a company

Tell how long (7 years)

Tell how long (4 months)

Ask if the two of them get along

VOCABULARY REVIEW

WORKPLACES

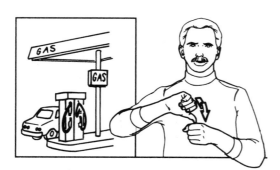

HOSPITAL RELATED ACTIVITIES

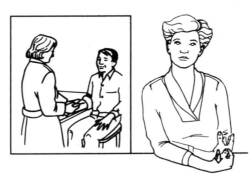

OCCUPATIONS

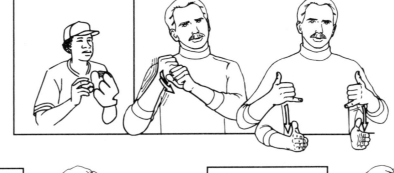

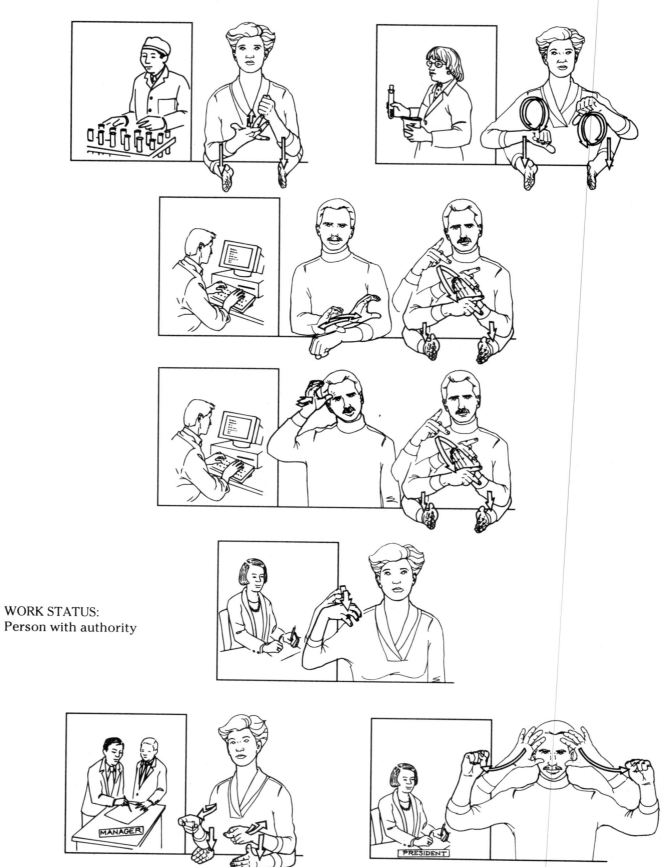

WORK STATUS:
Person with authority

EMPLOYMENT STATUS

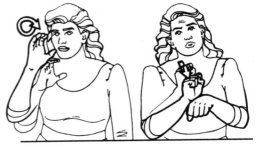

TELL HOW PEOPLE
GET ALONG

TELL HOW PEOPLE
DO NOT GET ALONG

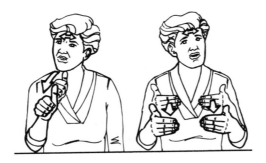

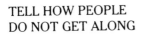

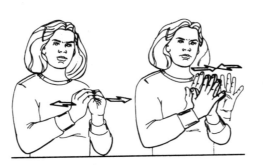

PRONOUNS

"two of us"   "two of them"

"any of them"   "all of them"

"they"

AGE NUMBERS

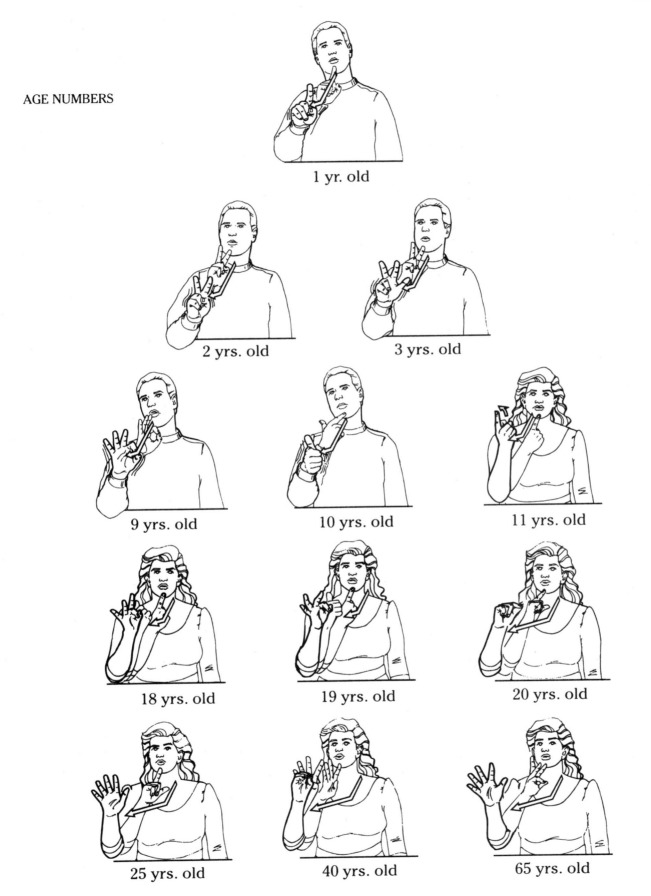

1 yr. old

2 yrs. old

3 yrs. old

9 yrs. old

10 yrs. old

11 yrs. old

18 yrs. old

19 yrs. old

20 yrs. old

25 yrs. old

40 yrs. old

65 yrs. old

Unit 11
Attributing Qualities to Others

LANGUAGE IN ACTION

Conversation 1

Ken (A) asks Mary (B) about a professor that he will have next semester.

A: tell B that you plan to take a class with a certain professor, ask if B has had that professor before
B: respond affirmatively
A: **ask B's opinion** of the professor
B: give opinion, **describe him (appearance, personality and behavior traits)**
A: respond; ask if you would like the teacher
B: assure A, but tell what A must do to pass the course
A: respond

Conversation 2

Ella (B) is studying in a student lounge. Cinnie (A) enters. She has just met a famous movie star.

A and B: greet each other
A: express excitement, tell news, check if B knows who you mean
B: affirm
A: **give your impression of her personality**
B: **disagree**, tell what you read about her
A: express doubt, ask which newspaper
B: give name of newspaper
A: give opinion of newspaper, **correct popular opinion of the person**
B: respond

Key phrases that express target language functions are highlighted. Replay the videotape until you can follow the conversations without the aid of the cues. Then rehearse both conversations, especially the key phrases.

CONVERSATION PRACTICE

To practice the key phrases in a new context, find a partner and role play the situations below:

Situation 1: You and a friend are reminiscing about memorable teachers you've had. Talk about three teachers and include the following about each one:

- physical descriptions
- positive and negative attributes
- any peculiarities in manner

Situation 2: You just read an article about a notable person that suggests s/he isn't what s/he appears to be. Summarize the article to your partner.

GRAMMAR NOTES

Numbers: 67-98

Some of the numbers 67 - 98 are unique in their forms because of the twisting movement of the wrist. For the first set of numbers, 67, 68, 69, 78, 79, 89, the wrist twists one way. For the second set of numbers, 76, 86, 87, 97, 98, the wrist twists the other way.

On screen, Brian will model both sets of numbers. Pay attention to the wrist movement, and where the number begins and where it ends. Go back and review this section frequently to practice reading these numbers; they are the hardest numbers to read.

Role Shifting

Role shifting occurs when a signer describes a person or character, tells what a person did or said, or shows how a person thinks or feels. This is done by "assuming the role" of that person and adopting his/her manner while recounting what was said or done.

In the classroom you have been introduced to one form of role shifting. You learned to adopt the manner and facial expressions associated with specific attributes, such as shyness, anger, humility, boldness.

There are more complex ways of using role shifting where whole conversations are represented. Role shifting makes the recounting of interaction clearer and more interesting. Role shifting is not just a style; it is the "way of telling" preferred in the Deaf community.

You will see examples of role shifting on screen in the three signed narratives that follow. Notice especially how the signer's eye gaze and head position shift, s/he assumes a role. (To see more examples of role shifting, replay any of the videotaped narratives.)

GRAMMAR PRACTICE

Describing Characters

Ben, Cinnie, and Mary will describe major characters from three classic films, *The Ten Commandments*, *The Sound of Music* and *Gone With the Wind*. Observe how they use role shifting when describing each character.

After each narrative, stop the tape and write down the name of each character described, then write the characteristic that best describes each one.

The Ten Commandments

Characters	Characteristics
Pharoh	mean, arrogant, rich
Jewish Slaves	scared, complain
Moses	good, humble, smart, brave

The Sound of Music

Characters	Characteristics
Baron Von Trap	handsome, stern
Von Trap Kids	scared, rude, mischevious
Maria	sweet, pretty, innocent, soft-hearted
Nazi Soldiers	evil, mean

Gone With the Wind

Characters	Characteristics
Scarlet O'Hara	beautiful, strong, snobbish
Ashley Wilks	handsome, coward, dependent
Melanie Wilks	sweet, friendly, strong, ~~compas~~
Rhett Butler	arrogant, bright, independent, gentleman

Practice role shifting by imitating the narrators' descriptions of the characters.

Answers on page 183.

PAIR PRACTICE

Think of five famous people and describe them to your partner as if you've forgotten their names. Follow the guidelines for describing people given in Unit 8, and use role shifting when describing personality, mannerisms, or things the person has said or done. Continue until your partner recognizes the person and spells the name.

COMPREHENSION

Winning Numbers

Try your luck. We'll give you not one chance, but *five* chances to win!

Watch the characters on screen as they announce the winning numbers (all numbers are between 50 and 100). Stop the tape and write the numbers below. After filling in all the numbers, check them with the Answer Key (page 182). Count how many numbers you read correctly, and write the number correct in the column on the right.

	Winning Numbers	Number Correct
Game 1.	66 53 98 76 89	4
Game 2.	88 76 59 87 64	3
Game 3.	55 83 57 69 73	5
Game 4.	77 67 98 91 97	5
Game 5.	99 78 52 96 68	4

Answer on page 183.

A Fishy Story

Ron tells a story about two good friends, Bob and Jack, who grew up in the same town. They both love to go fishing. Jack has great luck, while Bob never catches anything.

This narrative tells about Bob's many attempts to find the secret of Jack's success. Summary given on page 183. Bob buys same fishing pole as Jack. Asked Jack if they could switch places where they fish. Bob thought it was Jack's clothes that made him successful. He snuck into Jack's house, took his fishing clothes, fishing pole, and his worms. Bob went to Jack's fishing area and started fishing. Fish came out of water and said "You're not Jack! Where's Jack?" Bob was surprised and dropped his pole.

End of Unit 11

141

KEY PHRASES

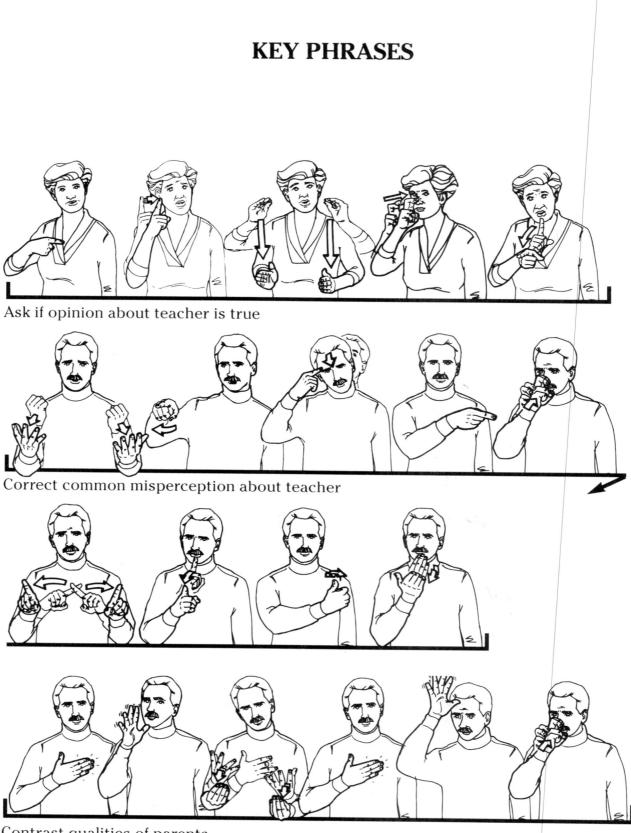

Ask if opinion about teacher is true

Correct common misperception about teacher

Contrast qualities of parents

142

VOCABULARY REVIEW

opposites

PERSONAL QUALITIES

 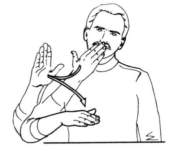

opposites

good/bad
rich/poor
young/old
strong/weak
happy/sad
strict/flexible
mean/soft heart
fast/slow
humble/arrogant
show off
Scared/tough

lazy/hard working
polite/rude
snob/friendly
famous/not
indepent/dependent
jealous
cute

pretty, handsome
ugly
smart, wise
shy, naive
strange
stupid/silly

opposites

PERSONAL QUALITIES
ATTRIBUTED TO
CHARACTERS IN

*"Snow White and
the Seven Dwarfs"*

Snow White

Stepmother

Prince

Doc

Sleepy

Grumpy

Happy

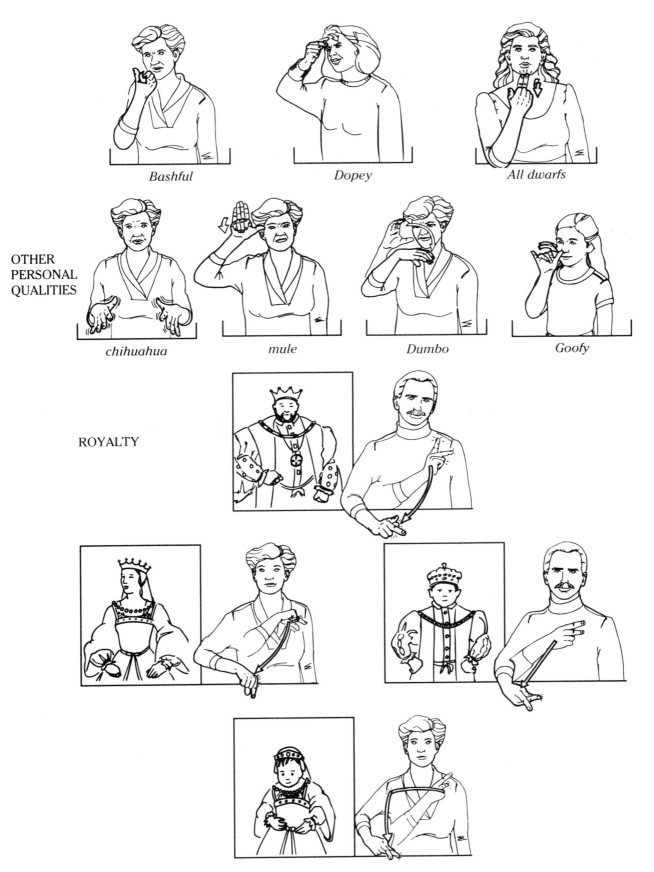

Bashful

Dopey

All dwarfs

OTHER PERSONAL QUALITIES

chihuahua

mule

Dumbo

Goofy

ROYALTY

PETS

NUMBERS
(twist to left)

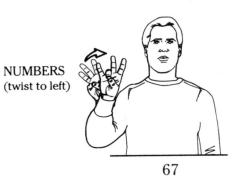

67

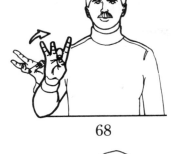

68

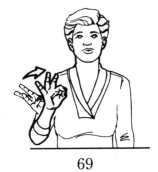

69

78

79

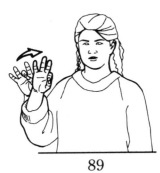

89

NUMBERS
(twist to right)

76

86

87

96

97

98

* If you are left-handed, movements are reversed.

Unit 12
Talking About Routines

LANGUAGE IN ACTION

Conversation

Mary (A) and her husband Ron (B) are at home. Mary is talking on the TTY with an Avon salesperson who wants to make an appointment to meet with them.

A: get husband's attention, **explain situation, ask when** salesperson can come
B: suggest Wednesday night
A: remind B of other plans for that night (PTA meeting)
B: suggest another night and time that week
A: describe routine, agree
B: respond
A: (return to TTY), **explain situation** with salesperson, ask if a later time that night would be OK
B: agree, but express condition (you go to bed at 11 p.m.)
A: (return to TTY) tell B that it is OK (end phone conversation)
B: (suddenly remember, wave to get attention)
A: (hang up phone, look at B)
B: tell A that her parents are coming to visit that night
A: respond, (dial phone again)

Key phrases that express target language functions are highlighted. Replay the videotape until you can follow the conversation without the aid of the cues. Then rehearse the conversation, especially the key phrases.

CONVERSATION PRACTICE

To practice the key phrases in a new context, find a partner and role play the situation below:

Situation: There has been a big change in your life. Discuss with your partner how this has changed your routine. (Possible changes: you got married, had a baby, got a new puppy, started a new job, broke your leg, your grandmother moved in.)

GRAMMAR NOTES

Clock Numbers

To tell the time from 1 to 12 o'clock, first sign "time" (index finger taps the wrist of the non-dominant hand), then sign the number indicating the hour.

For 1 - 9 o'clock, the number is signed with a slight waving movement in the fingerspelling area of the signing space. The numbers for 10, 11, and 12 o'clock are signed without the waving movement.

For 1 - 9 o'clock, the sign combination "time" + number is often contracted so that the number indicating the hour begins at the wrist of the non-dominant hand, and then moves to the fingerspelling area.

Hour and Minute Information. For combinations of hour and minute information, sign the number for the hour, then slightly to the right of that, sign the number for minutes. (Left-handed signers sign minutes slightly to the left.) There is no waving movement, and the sign for "time" does not usually precede the numbers. For the first nine minutes (:01 - :09), sign ZERO then the number, i.e.:

7:05 = SEVEN, ZERO FIVE.

Numbers 1 - 9 are signed with the palm facing away from the body for both hour and minute information; the rest of the numbers are signed just like the cardinal (or counting) numbers.

GRAMMAR PRACTICE

Clock Numbers

Ella will now model clock numbers on screen. Notice the direction her palm faces, the waving movement for numbers 1 - 9, and how she gives combined hour and minute information. Replay the tape and practice each number sign.

CALENDAR, PART 2

Cinnie will model four sentences saying when and how often an activity occurs. Two sentences indicate every week on the same day (i.e., "every Tuesday"). The other sentences indicate every day in the week, the same part of the day (i.e., "every evening next week"). See how the calendars below are marked to indicate the information given in each sentence.

For this activity, today is the *16th of the month*.

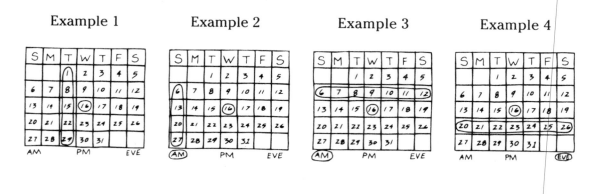

Example 1   Example 2   Example 3   Example 4

Activity. Brian will now sign four sentences saying when and how often activities occur. Mark the calendars to indicate the information given. Circle the part of the day if it is given.

1.   **2.**   **3.**   **4.**

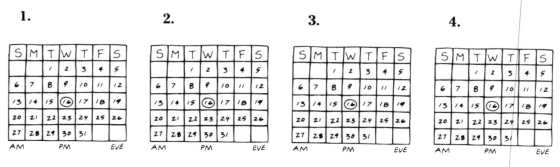

Answers on page 183.

Now rewind the tape and practice signing the sentences. Pay attention to the order in which the time information is given.

COMPREHENSION

What Time?

On screen several signers will tell you what they did at specific times. After each sentence, stop the tape and record the time, circle the part of the day, and write in the activity below.

Example:

time: __8:30__   (a.m.)   p.m.   eve.   activity: __get dressed__

time: _____   a.m.   p.m.   eve.   activity: _____

time: _____   a.m.   p.m.   eve.   activity: _____

time: _____   a.m.   p.m.   eve.   activity: _____

time: _____   a.m.   p.m.   eve.   activity: _____

time: _____   a.m.   p.m.   eve.   activity: _____

time: _____   a.m.   p.m.   eve.   activity: _____

time: _____   a.m.   p.m.   eve.   activity: _____

time: _____   a.m.   p.m.   eve.   activity: _____

Answers on pages 183, 184.

Safe Keeping

Mary tells a story about a woman hiding money in a safe place, but then forgetting where she put it. She goes on to tell how the woman and her husband searched for the money.

How much money did the woman hide? _____

List all the places the couple looked for the money: _____

_____

_____

Where did they finally find the money? _____

Summary given on page 184.

CULTURE/LANGUAGE NOTES
Brief History of Deaf America

In 1817 Laurent Clerc, a Deaf teacher from the National Royal Institution for the Deaf in Paris, came to the United States to help Thomas H. Gallaudet, a hearing American, start America's first School for the Deaf in Hartford, Connecticut. Clerc brought from the Paris school a highly effective teaching method using Sign Language, the language of Deaf people.

Graduates of the Hartford School went on to establish similar residential Schools for the Deaf in other states. Many Deaf people became teachers of the Deaf and Sign Language was the language of instruction in the classroom. Then in 1864, the first university for the Deaf (now called Gallaudet University) was established by a charter signed by President Lincoln.

Late in the 19th century the tide began to turn against Deaf people and their language. In 1880, the International Congress on Education of the Deaf in Milan, Italy adopted a resolution banning the use of Sign Language in teaching deaf children. The "oral method" of teaching gained momentum; speech and lipreading became the primary educational goal. Deaf people were discouraged from entering the teaching profession, and Sign Language was no longer permitted in the classroom.

Also in 1880 the National Association of the Deaf (NAD) was founded in Cincinnati, Ohio. This organization brought Deaf people together from around the country to work for their common interests and fight discrimination in schools and workplaces. Around the turn of the century, because of a growing concern that American Sign Language would be lost, the NAD established a fund used to make a series of films in Sign Language. One of these films is George Veditz's *Preservation of Sign Language*. Over the years, the NAD has fought public ignorance of deafness, underemployment of Deaf people, discrimination against Deaf people who were denied driver's licenses, discrimination against Deaf teachers, double tax exemption for Deaf people, and the strictly oral method in education of the Deaf.

The years from 1900 to 1960 could be considered the "Dark Ages" of Deaf history. What sustained the community during this period of strong oralism and lack of social understanding was the Deaf clubs. Local clubs provided a place where Deaf people could congregate to socialize, share the latest news, organize around political issues, plan events and outings, and, in later years, watch captioned films. The clubs nourished the sense of group loyalty and community, maintained the culture, and preserved the cherished language.

In 1901 the National Fraternal Society of the Deaf (NFSD) was formed to provide insurance to Deaf people. Initially providing burial benefits to members, the "Frat" expanded to include life, sickness, and accident insurance, and later fought discrimination against Deaf drivers in getting automobile insurance.

Through the years of the First World War and the depression, attempts to improve Deaf people's lives were not given priority, as was true for most minority groups. During the 1940's, however, the NAD was successful in getting the Civil Service Commission to revoke a ruling that discriminated against Deaf printers, making lucrative positions available to many Deaf people. During World War II, many Deaf people became "soldiers on the assembly line,"* performing a large variety of jobs and demonstrating that the abilities of Deaf people can contribute to any work force.

The 1960's ushered in an era of change, as evidenced by the following milestones:

- Teletypewriters for the Deaf (TTYs) were invented by a deaf man in 1964 and began to take hold during the 1970's. Later, with the invention of telecaption decoders, television too became accessible to deaf people.

- The National Registry of Interpreters for the Deaf was founded in 1964, leading to increased respect for, and greater proficiency within, the profession.

- The first linguistic study of American Sign Language was published in 1965. The study was made by William Stokoe at Gallaudet and had great impact on continued research and recognition of ASL.

- The educational philosophy of "Total Communication" began to gain acceptance, and signs were again permitted in the schools.

- In 1966, the NAD fought for the right of a Deaf couple in California to adopt a foster child. The judge had said that the child would not have a normal home environment with Deaf parents. After an outpouring of support from the Deaf communities all over the U.S., the couple was awarded custody of the child.

- The National Theatre of the Deaf first toured in 1967, spreading awareness and appreciation of ASL throughout the world.

- Section 504 of the Rehabilitation Act of 1973 (often called the civil rights act for disabled people) was finally signed into law in 1976. This law requires that any institution receiving federal funds be accessible to all disabled people. Sign Language interpreting services began to be provided at many colleges around the country, as well as in hospitals, courtrooms, government agencies and various workplaces.

---

*Jack R. Gannon, *Deaf Heritage: A Narrative History of Deaf America*, National Association of the Deaf, Silver Spring, Maryland, 1981, p. 222. For more information on the history of Deaf America, see Gannon's book and other NAD publications, as well as Harlan Lane, *When The Mind Hears: A History of the Deaf*, Random House, NY, 1984.

• In 1979, when the movie Voices was produced featuring a hearing performer in the role of a Deaf character, Deaf people staged a successful boycott of the movie in several cities, forcing the distributor to withdraw the film from the market. Since then, Deaf performers have become more visible on television, stage, and film, and Deaf people are more often hired to perform in Deaf roles.

In recent years, there has been increased academic acceptance of American Sign Language in colleges and universities. There has also been a growing recognition of Deaf culture by the general public. Deaf individuals are beginning to attain decision-making positions where they can make a difference in the lives of Deaf people. The "Deaf President Now" rally at Gallaudet University in the spring of 1988 drew widespread support not only from members of the Deaf community, but from many people in all walks of life. What happened at Gallaudet that fateful week was the culmination of a people's struggle to break the chains of paternalism. This struggle for Deaf rights and self-determination continues. The protest at Gallaudet is seen by many as the beginning of a new chapter in the life of Deaf America.

End of Unit 12

KEY PHRASES

Ask what time person usually gets up

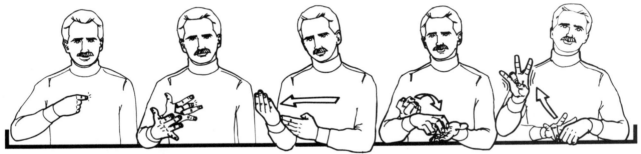

Tell what time you usually get up

Tell what you do every Tuesday

Tell what you do once a month

Tell about your morning routine

Ask what is a good time to go

VOCABULARY REVIEW

MORNING
ROUTINE

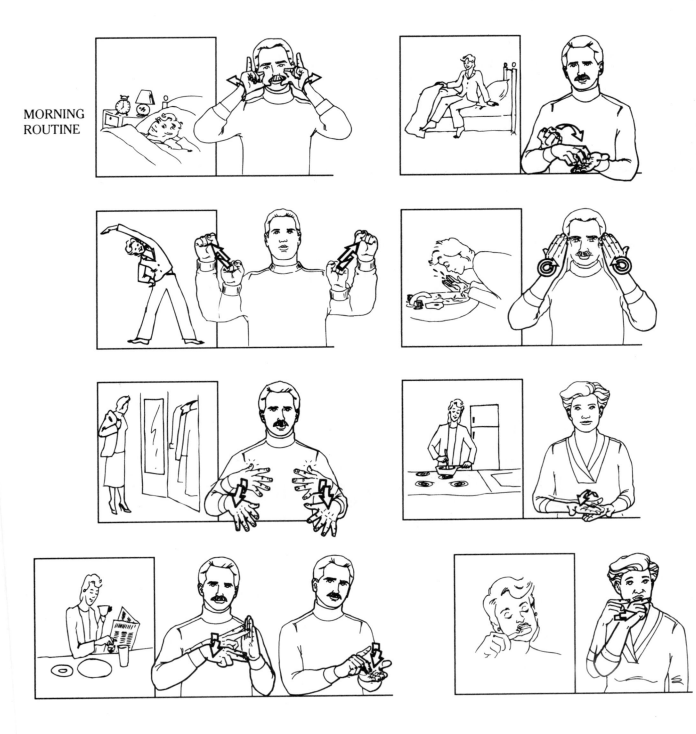

EVENING ROUTINE

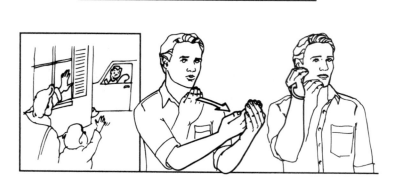

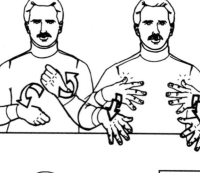

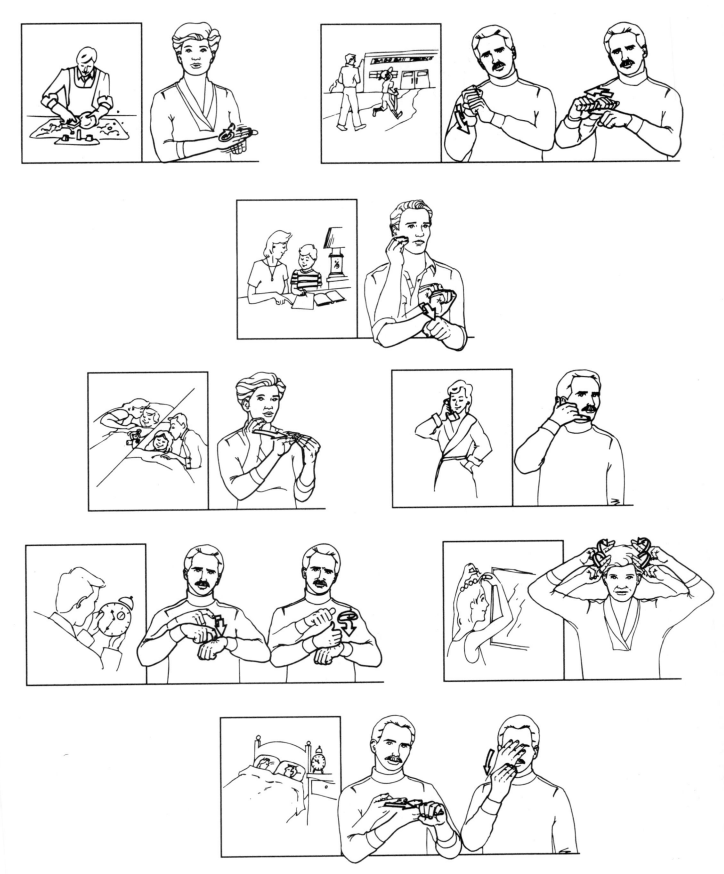

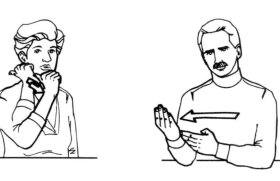

TIME SIGNS
Frequency

HOW OFTEN

always   never

LENGTH OF TIME

BEFORE/AFTER

APPROXIMATE TIME
(around 8:00)

WAYS TO WAKE UP

GETTING
READY

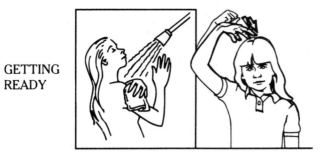

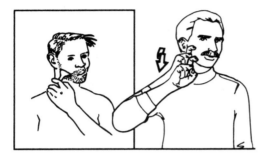

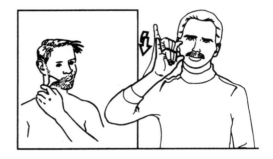

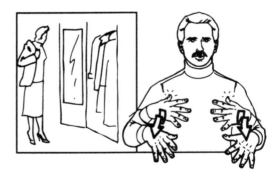

ROOMS IN THE HOUSE

WH-WORD
QUESTION SIGNS

CLOCK NUMBERS

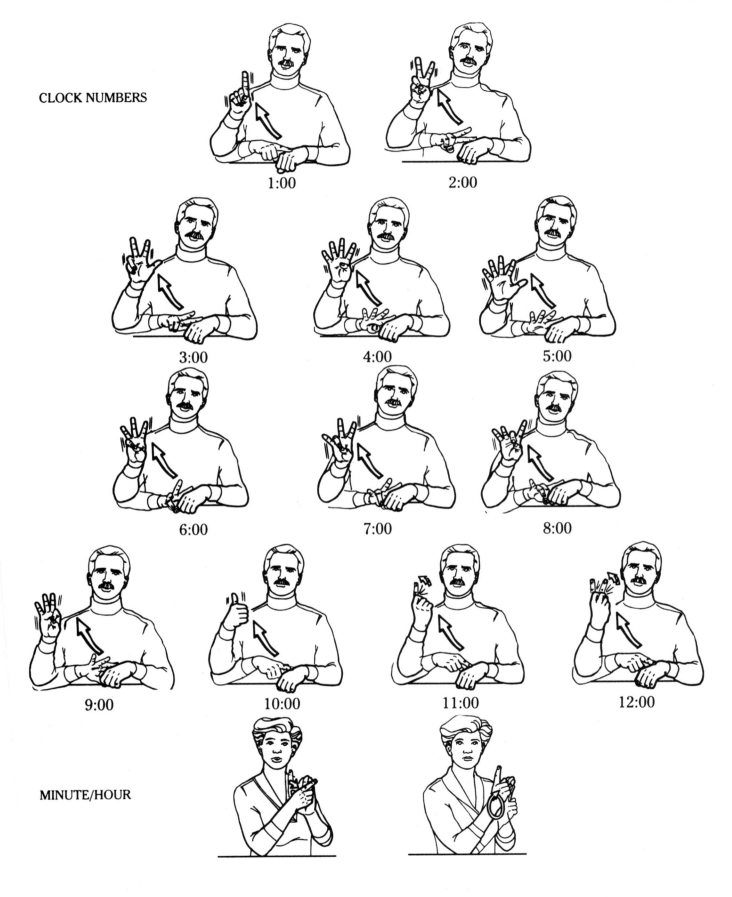

1:00

2:00

3:00

4:00

5:00

6:00

7:00

8:00

9:00

10:00

11:00

12:00

MINUTE/HOUR

Units 7 – 12
Cumulative Review

LANGUAGE AND CULTURE

Interrupting Conversations

On screen you will see several situations which focus on acceptable ways to interrupt conversations. Observe the attention-getting behaviors and phrases used to begin the interruptions. (These scenes were filmed in an informal situation, among people who know each other. Interrupting behaviors would vary in other situations.)

After you view the situations, read the summary of culturally appropriate behaviors that follows.

SUMMARY NOTES

When you are in situations where you know the people involved, you can interrupt conversations the ways you saw on screen. Otherwise, you may want to wait until you are acknowledged before interrupting.

How do you know when it's an appropriate time to interrupt a conversation? Some situations are obvious - while interruptions are commonplace at parties or social events, we are expected not to interrupt private conversations. Unfortunately, most situations are less obvious. The interrupter needs to look for clues to decide when to interrupt. For example, consider where the signers are in relation to other people (i.e., standing with their backs to others), the seriousness of the conversation, and the urgency of your message.

How do you interrupt a conversation? The approach you use depends on the situation. If it is a casual conversation, you may walk right up and get the attention of the person you wish to speak to by waving or touching his/her shoulder. If the conversation looks intense or you're unsure of the appropriateness of the interruption, then stand and wait at a polite distance to indicate that you are waiting for a chance to talk.

Once the signer acknowledges you, apologize for the interruption and explain why you wanted the person's attention. The signer may acknowledge you but ask you to wait for a second; you should then wait for eye contact that indicates it's your turn.

Handling Auditory Interruptions. In Dialogue 4 of the classroom videotape, a Deaf man was talking with the hearing receptionist at a Deaf service agency when the phone rang. The receptionist handled the interruption by asking the man to wait, informing him that the phone was ringing, and asking the caller to hold. She was then able to resume the conversation.

It is important to develop your skill in handling auditory interruptions, as they may occur frequently while you interact with Deaf people. If you are involved in a conversation and break eye contact because you hear the phone ring or someone calls your name, you should **inform the Deaf person** why you looked away. Simply say, "just a sec, the telephone " or "excuse me, someone's knocking on the door," etc. This way the Deaf person knows why you looked away.

knocking on the door," etc. This way the Deaf person knows why you are distracted and can adjust to the information. Breaking eye contact without an explanation is considered rude; it looks like you are inattentive or not interested in the conversation.

Closing Conversations

On screen, you will see Mary and Ella modeling phrases to use in ending conversations. Practice these phrases.

PAIR PRACTICE

Practice the behaviors you saw on screen by role playing the following situations with two other people:

Situation 1: At a party, the host is explaining something to someone. You need to ask the host if s/he has more 7-Up (or where you can find a bottle opener).

Situation 2: A friend is giving you instructions on how to get to the nearest ice cream store. Your 10-year-old son taps you excitedly in order to show you something he has found in the backyard. You tell him to wait until your friend finishes talking.

Situation 3: You're talking with your friend Jane on the phone. It so happens that Jane knows Willie, the Deaf person you work with, and wishes him to contact her.

Willie is talking with another person in the far corner of the room. Interrupt them to explain the situation and to ask for Willie's phone number so you can give it to Jane.

Situation 4: Two Deaf friends are having a serious discussion in the far corner of the room near a door. Inform them that someone is knocking at the door.

Situation 5: Ask the person sitting in the middle of the couch to get Judy's attention. (Judy is sitting next to the person, reading the newspaper.) Then ask Judy what time a certain movie is playing.

Situation 6: You and a Deaf woman are standing in the middle of the sidewalk in a park. The woman is telling you about her weekend when you see a person on rollerskates approaching. The Deaf woman is not aware that the skater is about to pass her. Interrupt to caution her.

Situation 7: You're having a great conversation with a person at a party, but you need to go home because the babysitter is expecting you. Explain to your friend that you have to leave now.

Situation 8: You've been talking with a friend for quite a while, and you need to make a phone call. Excuse yourself but tell your friend you'll be right back.

Situation 9: You're just finishing a conversation, but before you go, check with your friend to confirm the dinner appointment for next Wednesday night.

GRAMMAR PRACTICE

Analyzing Numbers

On screen, several signers will sign sentences incorporating a number sign. After each sentence, write down the number and circle the number type.

Number		*Number Type*			
1._____	cardinal	cents	age	clock	ordinal
2._____	cardinal	cents	age	clock	ordinal
3._____	cardinal	cents	age	clock	ordinal
4._____	cardinal	cents	age	clock	ordinal
5._____	cardinal	cents	age	clock	ordinal
6._____	cardinal	cents	age	clock	ordinal
7._____	cardinal	cents	age	clock	ordinal
8._____	cardinal	cents	age	clock	ordinal
9._____	cardinal	cents	age	clock	ordinal
10._____	cardinal	cents	age	clock	ordinal
11._____	cardinal	cents	age	clock	ordinal
12._____	cardinal	cents	age	clock	ordinal
13._____	cardinal	cents	age	clock	ordinal
14._____	cardinal	cents	age	clock	ordinal
15._____	cardinal	cents	age	clock	ordinal

Answers on page 184.

Questions to Ask

Now that you are at the end of Level 1, you should be able to ask the following questions. Read the cue for each question, think about how you would ask it, and watch Cinnie model the question on screen. Then find a partner and practice signing the questions (and answers) to each other.

1. ask if the other person has already eaten

2. offer to bring the other person something to drink

3. ask the other person if she wants to go out to eat with you

4. ask the other person where s/he works

5. ask the other person to describe what s/he does at work

6. ask the other person how old his/her father is

7. ask the other person what time the two of you will meet at the movie theatre next Tuesday

8. ask the other person what color Ian's new car is

9. ask the other person how many brother and sisters s/he has

10. ask the other person where s/he ranks among siblings

11. ask if what you heard about a physician is true

12. ask the other person how long his/her parents have been married

13. ask the other person how long s/he has been working as a carpenter

14. ask the other person what s/he and his/her friend will be doing at a specific time on a specific day

15. ask the other person when his/her daughter's birthday is

16. ask the other person if an item in the room belongs to him/her

17. ask how the other person is getting to a party next Saturday night

18. ask if directions to a particular location are correct

19. ask the other person how s/he gets along with his/her boss

20. identify and describe someone in the room, then ask the other person who s/he is

CULTURE/LANGUAGE NOTES

Maintaining Continuity in Relationships

One day, a Deaf woman was invited to a beginning ASL class. The instructor introduced the woman by giving information about her community ties and her personal life. Then students were asked to introduce themselves, and include information such as marital status, number of children, line of work, and any other personal comments. The visitor chatted briefly about these things with each student. (There were about twenty students in the class.) After the last student introduced herself, she jokingly said to the visitor, "That's a lot to remember." The visitor replied, "I remember most of it," and proceeded to amaze the class by going around the room restating information about each student, pointing out similarities between students' lives, and recalling personal comments.

The students thought the visitor had an exceptional memory. The instructor explained, however, that she possessed no extraordinary talent, but rather reflected a learned cultural

171

behavior. She had done what most Deaf persons do naturally she attended to information that establishes a person's community ties, that assists her in identifying that person to others in the community, and that helps her maintain continuity in the relationship (or in this case the "acquaintanceship").

Deaf culture is called a "high-context" culture. Deaf people have an extensive information-sharing network among families, friends, and community members, and are involved in a host of familiar relationships. Among Deaf people, there is a great deal of shared knowledge, common experiences, goals and beliefs, common friends and acquaintances, a common way of talking; that is, their lives share a common context.

When two Deaf people meet for the first time, they establish this context by giving information about their community ties. They attend to specific information and retain it. When they meet again, they expect each other to remember their previous exchange and will begin to talk from that basis. Each will learn a little more about the other, which in turn will be remembered. This maintains continuity not only in that relationship; the information is fed back into the information-sharing network to help contextualize each person in relationship to the overall fabric of the community.

As you begin to meet Deaf people in and out of the classroom, you should volunteer information about yourself and make a point of retaining relevant information about others. The next time you meet, you should be able to recall the information exchanged in the first meeting, and from that context begin to build a relationship. Your ability to maintain continuity in relationships depends on your ability to remember relevant information about people. This developed skill will allow you to understand and participate in conversational patterns common in the Deaf community.

Deaf Awareness Quiz

Go back to the Deaf Awareness Quiz on p. viii and re-evaluate your answers. Correct answers are provided in the Answer Key on page 184.

End of Cumulative Review: Units 7–12

KEY PHRASES

Interrupting conversation

Interrupting conversation to relay a message

Ending a conversation (phrase 1)

Ending a conversation (phrase 2)

Ending a conversation (phrase 3)

Ask to hold conversation

Ask how much it costs

VOCABULARY REVIEW

WAYS TO ASK FOR
CLARIFICATION

WAYS TO GIVE
FEEDBACK AND
COMMENTS

ANSWER KEY

UNIT 1

Same or Different

Sentence Types:

1. S	6. D
2. D	7. S
3. D	8. S
4. S	9. D
5. D	10. D

Shapes:

11. D
12. D
13. S
14. S
15. D

Sequencing:

16. D
17. D
18. S
19. D
20. S

UNIT 2

Question Types

1. wh	6. y/n
2. wh	7. y/n
3. y/n	8. wh
4. wh	9. wh
5. y/n	10. y/n

Number Phrases

1. 7,10	6. 9,6
2. 1,3	7. 5,4
3. 6,2	8. 3,8
4. 3,6	9. 4,7
5. 10,5	10. 8,9

UNIT 3

Identify Where

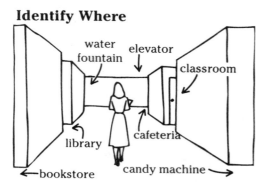

Picture It

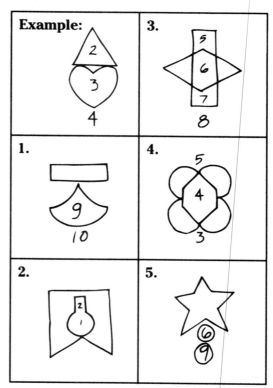

Fingerspelling, Part 1

	Brian	Cinnie	Ron
1.	X		
2.			X
3.		X	
4.			X
5.	X		
6.	X		
7.		X	
8.			X
9.		X	
10.		X	

UNIT 4

Grid Game

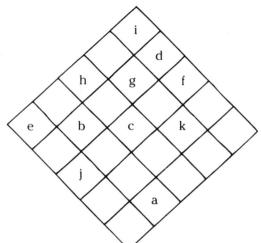

Ben's Keys

1. 12 keys altogether
2. 5 keys for the apartment
   1 key for the padlock
   3 keys for the car
   1 key for the bicycle lock
   2 keys for work
3. in the classroom
4. lives in New York

Trivia #1

15 + 2 = E
14 + 8 = R
10 + 19 = C
17 + 6 = N
1 + 20 = E
16 + 4 = A
6 + 12 = L
19 + 8 = R
3 + 13 = T
9 + 16 = L
11 + 4 = U
6 + 18 = C

Answer: Laurent Clerc

UNIT 5

Bob and Bill

Bob

met wife in college
has 1 sister
lives in a house
studying English
gets here by bus
deaf

Bill

met wife in high school
has 3 sisters
lives in an apartment
studying French
drives a car
hearing

Ten Years Later. . .

had litter of ten kittens
now dead

deceased

gave birth to a boy who is deaf,
the boy is now nine years old

studying Sign Language
bought a big house

grown up, now in high school
has a boyfriend

still living

married, now divorced
attending college
studying French

Fingerspelling, Part 2

1. Tom	6. Kris
2. Sue	7. Judy
3. Ben	8. Jesse
4. Sean	9. Glenn
5. Mona	10. Bobby

A Riddle

The bus driver made 5 stops.

UNIT 6

Calendar, Part 1

1. 16th, eve
2. 24th, p.m.
3. 15th, p.m.
4. 1st, eve
5. 16th, a.m.
6. 18th, p.m.
7. 9th, a.m.
8. 14th, eve
9. 17th, a.m.
10. 2nd, eve
11. 19th, p.m.

Main Street, USA

1. apartment building
2. Somerset Apartments
3. church
4. Jack's Steak House
5. City Hospital
6. Sears
7. Jack's Steak House

What Did They Decide?

Dialogue 1

next Tuesday

Dialogue 2

next Wednesday

Dialogue 3

next Friday

What Reasons Did They Give?

Dialogue 4
Reasons given: felt sick,
had to see a physician

Dialogue 5
Reasons given: was late because he
talked with friend, got stuck in traffic

Trivia #2

1. 19 - 12
2. 30 - 16
3. 24 - 4
4. 28 - 11
5. 15 - 14
6. 26 - 17
7. 27 - 21
8. 18 - 13
9. 20 - 9
10. 29 - 3
11. 25 - 22

Answer: George Veditz

CUMULATIVE REVIEW: UNITS 1-6

Sentence Types

1. statement
2. wh
3. statement
4. y/n
5. neg
6. wh
7. y/n
8. neg
9. statement
10. neg
11. wh
12. y/n

Which Room Was It?

Answer: He honked the horn of his car until the lights in all the rooms but one were turned on.

Summary: A Deaf couple on vacation decided to stop at a motel for the night. They were lucky to get the last room available. The husband left the motel office to go buy something to drink, while his wife got the key and went to the room. When the husband returned to the motel, he realized he did not know the room number. The lights in all the rooms were out. He pondered what to do next, then he thought of something. He honked the horn of his car until the lights in all the rooms but one were turned on. The one with the lights still off must be the right room.

UNIT 7

Fingerspelling, Part 3

1. ice
2. TV
3. diet
4. Coke
5. oil
6. fun
7. HS
8. apt
9. 7-Up
10. TTY
11. van
12. cake

The Candy Bar

A man went to the airport and stood in line to buy his ticket. When he got to the ticket counter he found out that his flight had been delayed. He decided to buy a newspaper, a candy bar and a cup of coffee. He found a seat, made himself comfortable and started reading the newspaper. He soon noticed the man sitting next to him take a bite of the candy bar. He was astonished, gave him a dirty look and then took a bite of the candy bar himself. The other man had the same reaction and popped the rest of the candy into his mouth. The first man was really furious, but just then, he heard it was time to board the plane. He got on the plane and sat down. After the plane took off, he reached into his back pocket to get a comb, and instead pulled out the candy bar that he had bought.

Personal Data

deaf

used to be
married, now
divorced

Jamie

likes to go to
the movies

Sean

has six
children

Missing Number
1. 40
2. 44
3. 60
4. 25
5. 70

UNIT 9

Give and Take

Who?	How Much?
1. Sally	none
2. Jane	35 cents
3. Bob	none
4. Bob	30 cents
5. Sally	30 cents

Making Requests

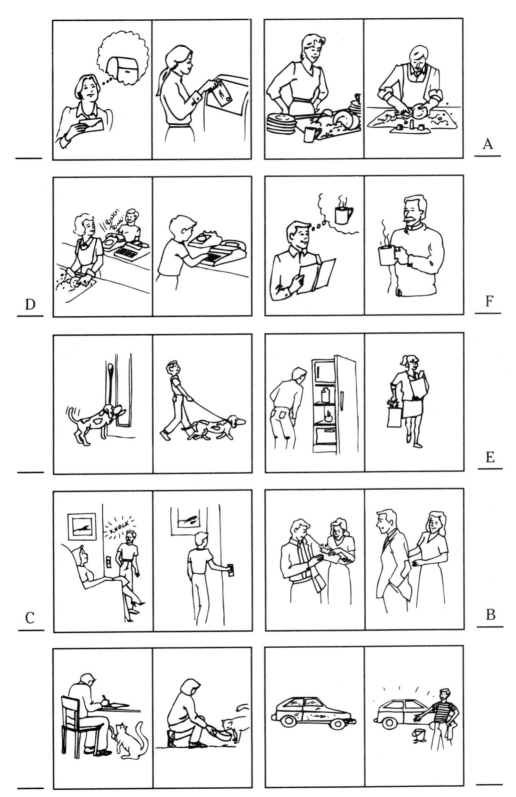

ABC Gum

After the boy stuck the gum on the bench and went home, a man sat on the bench to read a book. When he was ready to get up, he found the gum sticking to his pants. In disgust, he removed it and threw it on the sidewalk. A woman walked by and stepped on it. She removed it from her shoe and flung it at a tree where it stuck. Later, two young lovers came along and stopped under the tree. The girl leaned against the tree and the boy rested his hand against the trunk as he talked to her. Upon leaving, he pulled his hand away only to find it stuck to the gum. He pitched the gum onto the bench. Finally, the boy returned to find the gum in the same place. He popped it into his mouth and started blowing bubbles.

UNIT 10

Talking About Children

eldest: 36-year-old son — married, works as a printer
second: 33-year-old son — divorced, teaches at a state School for the Deaf
third: 31-year-old daughter — married, works with computers
fourth: 27-year-old daughter — single, works at a bank
fifth: 27-year-old son — separated, looking for a job
sixth: 24-year-old daughter — now attending college, has a steady boyfriend

A Show of Hands

1. Contestant 1 (standing closest to the game show host)
     her name is Carol
     her family is not present because they live far away
     she is not married
     she has two younger brothers
     she is a manager at a factory
   Contestant 2
     her name is Janie
     she is married
     she has four children:
        oldest is seven years old(girl),
        second oldest is six years old(girl),
        third is a four-year-old boy,
        the youngest is a three-year-old boy.
     she works as a lab technician at a hospital nearby
2. Name three Deaf publishers.
3. DawnSignPress, NAD, and Silent News
4. Name three well-known Deaf female artists
5. Betty Miller, Regina O. Hughes, and Linda Bove
6. Linda Bove, because she is an actress, not an artist
7. Linda Tom

Fingerspelling, Part 4

1. WI   5. NN
2. EE   6. ING
3. NT   7. GL
4. OY   8. GHT

UNIT 11

Describing Characters

The Ten Commandments

Characters	*Characteristics*
Pharaoh	cruel, arrogant, wealthy
Jewish slaves	fearful, complaining
Moses	good, humble, wise and courageous

The Sound of Music

Characters	*Characteristics*
Baron Von Trapp	good-looking, gentlemanly, stern
Von Trapp children	frightened (of Dad), rude (to Maria), mischievous
Maria	sweet, pretty, innocent, accepting, soft-hearted
The Nazis (soldiers)	evil, mean

Gone With the Wind

Characters	*Characteristics*
Scarlett O'Hara	beautiful, strong, independent, snobbish
Ashley Wilkes	handsome, cowardly, dependent on others
Melanie Wilkes	sweet, friendly, fragile but strong, homely handsome,
Rhett Butler	arrogant, boastful, bright, independent, gentlemanly

Winning Numbers

Game 1. 66, 53, 98, 79, 86
Game 2. 88, 76, 59, 87, 64
Game 3. 55, 83, 58, 69, 73
Game 4. 77, 67, 98, 91, 97
Game 5. 99, 78, 52, 96, 68

A Fishy Story

To figure out the secret of Jack's success, the first thing Bob did was to buy exactly the same kind of fishing pole that Jack used. To assure success he asked Jack if he could switch fishing spots with him. Bob then thought it might be Jack's clothes that did the trick. One day when Jack was away, Bob snuck into Jack's house, took his fishing outfit and his fishing pole, and even his worms. Bob then went to one of Jack's fishing spots, and started to fish. A fish came up out of the water and remarked "Hey, you're not Jack! Where's Jack?" Bob was so stunned he dropped the pole.

UNIT 12

Calendar, Part 2

1. Every Wednesday (2,9,16,23,30)
2. Every afternoon this week (14,15,16,17,18)
3. Each day at 12:00 noon next week (21,22,23,24,25)
4. Every Monday night (7,14,21,28)

What Time?

1. 9:45 eve, husband and I had a serious discussion
2. 7:15 a.m., made breakfast, then fed the cat
3. 6:15 eve, friend rings me up
4. 10:00 a.m., you go to your French class
5. 12:30 a.m., said goodbye, then left

6. 3:00 p.m., rooster crowing
7. 11:45 eve, get in bed
8. 4:30 p.m., help children with their homework

Safe Keeping

A married couple had been planning to go on vacation. The week before the trip, the husband asked his wife to withdraw a hundred dollars from the bank. After withdrawing the money, the woman decided to hide it in a safe place. As the vacation neared, the husband asked about the money, but she could not remember where she hid it. The two of them searched everywhere (under chair cushion, in every book on the shelves, under the lamp, on top of the dishes and inside the cups in the kitchen cabinets, under the mattress, inside the dresser drawers, and inside the pockets of the coat in the closet. Finally, the woman found the money behind a picture on the wall. Her husband told her he thought it was a lousy place to hide the money, and she retorted, "Lousy? Hmmph."

CUMULATIVE REVIEW: UNITS 7-12
Analyzing Numbers

1.	67	cardinal				
2.	5	cents	9.	8	ordinal	
3.	47	age	10.	10:45	clock	
4.	9:15	clock	11.	75	cents	
5.	2	ordinal	12.	2:30	clock	
6.	6	ordinal	13.	43	cardinal	
7.	29	age	14.	28	cents	
8.	60	cardinal	15.	15	age	

Deaf Awareness Quiz

1. d, f (see p. 3)
2. c (see pp. 3 and 154)
3. a, b (see p. 3)
4. a (see p. 81)
5. c (see p. 3)
6. a (see pp. 8, 19, 40, 90 and 139)
7. c (see pp. vii and 8)
8. b, d (see p. 33)
9. b, c, d (see pp. 19, 39, 52 and 108)
10. b (see p. 70)
11. c (see p. 70)
12. b, d (see pp. 59 and 81)
13. a (see p. 81)
14. a, b, d (see pp. 4, 59, 73, 154 and 171)
15. e (see p. 4)
16. a, b, c, e (see p. 154)
17. a, b, c (see p. 154)
18. c (see pp. 4 and 154)

End of Answer Key